A Guide to
Business Continuity Planning

A Guide to Business Continuity Planning

James C Barnes

WILEY

JOHN WILEY & SONS, LTD

Chichester • New York • Weinheim • Brisbane • Singapore • Toronto

This publication is designed to provide accurate and authoritative information in regard to the subject matter covered. It is sold on the understanding that the Publisher is not engaged in rendering professional services. If professional advice or other expert assistance is required, the services of a competent professional should be sought.

Other Wiley Editorial Offices

John Wiley & Sons Inc., 111 River Street, Hoboken, NJ 07030, USA

Jossey-Bass, 989 Market Street, San Francisco, CA 94103-1741, USA

Wiley-VCH Verlag GmbH, Boschstr. 12, D-69469 Weinheim, Germany

John Wiley & Sons Australia Ltd, 33 Park Road, Milton, Queensland 4064, Australia

John Wiley & Sons (Asia) Pte Ltd, 2 Clementi Loop #02-01, Jin Xing Distripark, Singapore 129809

John Wiley & Sons Canada Ltd, 22 Worcester Road, Etobicoke, Ontario, Canada M9W 1L1

British Library Cataloguing in Publication Data

A catalogue record for this book is available from the British Library

ISBN 0 471 53015 8

Typeset in 10/12pt Garamond by Dorwyn Ltd, Rowlands Castle, Hants
Printed and bound in Great Britain by Antony Rowe Ltd, Chippenham, Wiltshire
This book is printed on acid-free paper responsibly manufactured from sustainable forestry
in which at least two trees are planted for each one used for paper production.

Contents

Foreword

Since the late 1990s, the business continuity industry has evolved at a far more rapid pace than at any time since its birth in the 1970s. The industry focus has expanded far beyond early "glass-house" data center disaster recovery to the multinational, 24 × 7 enterprise dependent on pervasive computing and networking. The unforgiving nature of continuous availability of business and internet-based processes goes far beyond the technical complexities of recovering disrupted computing platforms or networks. "Traditional" disruption scenarios – such as hurricanes, fires, power outages or flooding have been supplanted with terrorism, denial-of-service attacks, workplace violence, and a host of other threats unimaginable two decades ago.

For any contingency planner to succeed requires a great deal of foresight and imagination – just consider what your organization's list of threats and vulnerabilities might look like in another twenty years – but it also requires some practical, day-to-day tools, structures and processes. In this book Jim Barnes has succeeded in providing us a much-needed tool, with which we can confidently face many of the day-to-day challenges of business contingency planning.

Pity the poor contingency planner – whether starting a consulting engagement, or delegated the daunting task of equipping an enterprise to survive and function in the face of disruption. How are they to tackle business continuity management? Where are they to begin? How do they anticipate and deal with project pitfalls along the way?

Whether volunteering or volunteered for the challenges of business continuity, they certainly should not have to reinvent the wheel. Yet, despite the wealth of books, software packages, periodicals, websites, conferences and seminars available, sometimes the success of a business continuity project can be more a result of utilizing a single, focused resource than bits and pieces from too many, disparate – and often contradictory – sources.

I have been actively involved with writing, editing and reviewing books and software tools in the business continuity industry for over seventeen years. During that time I have seen hundreds of strategies, methodologies, tools and tactics intended to make that contingency planner's job easy – or, as likely, miserable. From the most down-to-earth approach to the most elegant, I have observed that there is little consistency – and many contradictions. In addition, many of these approaches, while theoretically sound, have little bearing on the real world.

I have also found that the authors of too many books make naïve assumptions about the business continuity process. They assume that business continuity starts with all parties in agreement and, somehow, the laws of corporate nature do not apply to business continuity. Often, they treat the business continuity project as if it were something almost mystical – a process that somehow is exempt from the realities, constraints, processes, psychology and personalities of corporate or organizational life.

Jim Barnes, however, shares with us practical processes and tools that, as obvious as it may sound, treat the business continuity process just like any other enterprise implementation process. He addresses these processes to the individual or team who are going to have to deal with corporate rules, practices and realities, whether they are external consultants or internal staff.

Some books tell the reader to perform tasks and assume that the reader can figure out how to accomplish those tasks in the all-too-often, mercilessly unforgiving corporate environment. Instead, Jim Barnes has provided a practical framework including checklists, specific steps necessary for these tasks to take place at all, even examples of effective correspondence. For example, what is the point in teaching a contingency planner how to conduct a data-gathering interview until the interviewee agrees to participate willingly? With this book, Jim Barnes has taken an important step in removing much of the guesswork and frustration from the business continuity implementation project.

Philip Jan Rothstein, FBCI
President, Rothstein Associates Inc., publisher of *The Rothstein Catalog on Disaster Recovery*, 2001

pjr@rothstein.com

www.rothstein.com
Copyright © 2001, Rothstein Associates Inc. Used with permission.

1 Introduction

The interest in business continuity has gained significant momentum in the last several years, especially with the Y2K non-event. There are several reasons for this heightened interest, but probably the most significant reason is the increasing levels of devastation associated with recent disasters.

In recent years we have witnessed a series of headline-grabbing, thought-provoking disasters: hurricanes, power outages, floods, tornadoes, earthquakes, and ice and snow storms.

Because these disasters occupy prominent coverage by the news media, the senior management meetings of virtually every company and governmental entity eventually get around to discussing the prospect of a disaster interrupting their operations.

The magnitude of the natural disasters is not without precedent. Throughout time, Mother Nature has been delivering fierce hurricanes, horrific earthquakes, and devastating floods. Man-made disasters such as the burning of Rome, San Francisco, and Chicago have also been with mankind since the beginning of recorded history. What makes them different today is the density of our population and production centers.

The difference between yesterday's natural disasters and today's natural disasters is population density. What we have seen in all recent disasters is the impact of our dense population centers coping poorly with their environments or with the malevolent intentions of a disgruntled group of individuals.

The prognosis for an increasing toll from these forces is not good. We will continue to see an ever-increasing swath of destruction from the forces of nature and man.

While the above-mentioned disasters are spectacular, they are not the major causes of a disaster condition. Power outages have accounted for nearly one-third of all disaster conditions since 1982. Fire accounts for 5%. This is equal to the damage caused by storms, floods, hurricanes, and earthquakes. The major cause of the disaster condition is a localized occurrence that does not receive the attention of the awesome forces of nature. However, it can have just as great an impact on your company or organization.

The causes of a disaster condition are varied and numerous. There are at least 75 known causes for a disaster condition, from air conditioning failure to volcanoes, including such items as burst pipes, insect infestation, programmer error, toilet overflow, and chemical spills.

It is these more common occurrences—those that happen to an individual company as opposed to an entire area—that get the senior management of a company to take discussions beyond the point of "what if" to questions of "how can we prepare for this type of thing happening again?" Companies that are the most motivated to do something about disaster recovery are those that have recently had a disaster within their organization. This is a rather sad commentary, but most organizations are still reactive rather than proactive.

As a source of motivation for undertaking Business Continuity Planning, Table 1.1 gives a list of international requirements for producing a Business Continuity Plan (BCP).

The focus of this book is the building of a successful BCP. It is designed to provide you with proven tools and a sequential methodology that will allow you to succeed. It begins at the point where an organization has exhibited an interest in having a plan as a form of protection against a disaster and have asked you to develop a BCP.

This book has been written from the point of view of an outside consultant assisting a client to implement a plan. However, the intent was to give those inside an organization who have been tasked with developing a BCP insights on completing the project. Regardless of whether you are an external consultant or an internal project manager, the project methodology presented here will contribute significantly to your success.

THE STRUCTURE OF THE BOOK

The book follows the five phases of Business Continuity Planning:

- Project Foundation
- Business Assessment
- Strategy Selection
- Plan Development and
- Testing and Maintenance

Phases

It can be argued that there are more or less than five phases (every consulting firm will have its own magic number) but the core components contained in the phases should not vary. It is the dissection and explanation of each of these components that will make up the majority of this book. A grasp of all these components will enable you to develop an organizational BCP.

To assist you as you go through the book, Table 1.2 provides an explanation of each phase and its components.

Table 1.1 Disaster Recovery Preparedness Program: Regulatory Requirements

Country	Regulatory agency	Source	Requirements
USA	Federal Reserve FDIC OCC	1996 FFIEC IS Examination Handbook	• Obtain commitment of senior management • Establish a management group to monitor development and implementation of the plan • Perform a risk assessment: – Consider possible threats – Assess impacts from the loss of information (internally and externally) – Evaluate critical needs – Establish priorities based on critical needs – Determine strategies to recover – Obtain written backup agreements and/or contracts – Organize and document a written plan – Document strategies and procedures to recover – Develop procedures to execute the plan's priorities for critical vs. non-critical functions – Establish criteria for testing and maintenance of the plan – Determine conditions and frequency for testing – Establish procedures to revise and maintain the plan – Provide training for personnel involved in plan execution – Present the contingency plan to senior management/board for approval – Store a copy of the plan off-site with other reserve supplies
	NYSE (NY Stock Exchange)	212–656–3000	No published requirements on disaster recovery or business continuity plan, but members are examined for compliance with SEC regulations.
	New York State Banking Department	212–618–6642 option 5	No published requirements on disaster recovery or business continuity plan, but members are examined for compliance for emergency preparedness as stated by the SEC.

Country	Regulatory agency	Source	Requirements
USA (continued)	CFTC (Commodities and Futures Trading Commission)	CFTC 212–466–2061	The fieldwork of the CFTC focuses on the segregation of the client and firm capital. System and Planning Controls must be submitted in the Risk Assessment Filings that member firms file with the CFTC. There are no specific guidelines the CFTC follows when reviewing the Risk Assessment Filings; however, "best practices" in risk management internal control are often considered. These are culled from a variety of sources, including DPG, IOSCO and other regulators. They rely on the DSRO (Designated Self Regulation Organization) of the firms and the outside public accounting firms to evaluate these plans in detail
	NFA (National Futures Association)	NFA 212–608–8660	No published requirements on disaster recovery or BCPs but must be in compliance with overall NFA and CFTC rules and regulations.
	CBT (Chicago Board of Trade)	CBT 312–435–3500	No published requirements on disaster recovery or BCPs but must be in compliance with overall CBT rules and regulations.

	SEC (Securities and Exchange Commission)	"Contingency Planning Checklist" from Scott Aryan	• Policies
			  – Corporate and EDP policies on contingency planning are clear and consistent
			  – The organization has defined the possible emergency scenarios that it could suffer
			  – A formal contingency/disaster recovery plan is in place
			  – Staff are aware of contingency plans and policies
			• Action Plan
			  – Assumptions
			    • Contingency plans are procedures to follow to resolve system failures generally due to the following: processor errors, memory errors, communications network failure, peripheral device failure, operator error, applications program error, power failure, environmental failure, database erosion or failure, system saturation, and events such as fire and possible theft

- The contingency plan documentation should ensure that the following are appropriately identified: events that are included; events that are excluded; and the support commitments, such as funding or staff resources, underlying the plan
  - Responsibilities
- The appropriate staff levels of responsibility are assigned for the contingency situation
- The emergency chain of command is clear and easy to follow
- The Operations Management staff is clearly assigned responsibility under contingency conditions
  Shift Supervisors are aware of the scope of their responsibility
  - Strategy
- The contingency plan document includes the emergency responses that fall into clearly identified scenarios
- The backup operations are identifiable with a clear strategy such as mirrored, a standby, or a two production data center with split workload
- The procedures for recovery are consistent with the strategy selected
- All critical applications and hardware components have been identified and provided
- The timeframe to recover matches the optimal timeframe to recover as indicated by the business impact analysis loss curve
- The written emergency plan addresses the actions to be taken in specific emergency situations
- The disaster recovery plan includes: data and program

Country	Regulatory agency	Source	Requirements
USA (continued)			file backups and locations of such; remote storage of emergency procedures and manuals; input capture/ output distribution; on-line network backup; assignment of duties for reconstruction and off-site processing; decision responsibility to use the backup site; notification procedures for the provider of the backup facilities; transportation procedures for staff and data programs to the backup facilities; processing priorities
			– Record of Changes
			• The operations procedures ensure that: change sheets are updated to all environments; the distribution list for all related notification is up to date; software is compatible at all levels; any network can be switched; steps have been taken to reduce the possibility of human error; and backup job scheduling priorities are clearly defined
			– Preparatory Actions
			• *Personnel:* Staff assignments are reviewed to ensure that the following are maintained: there is a complete listing of assigned personnel with address, telephone, and/or beeper number; there are rosters of team composition; where Recovery Teams are identified, there is an accurate list for each Recovery Team; the written emergency plans address staffing and responsibilities of such; there is a notification sequence of employees as to declaration of a disaster
			• *Data:* On-site and off-site inventories are maintained; and critical files needed for backup site processing are clearly identified
			• *System and Application Software:* On-site and off-site inventories are maintained; a schedule of how and when they are updated is maintained

- *Hardware:* The following documentation is maintained: inventory list reflecting vendor name, address, and emergency contact, and an emergency acquisition agreement

- *Communications:* The communications contingency plans have the following: specific scenarios are defined; the current on-site requirements are easily accessible/maintained; and the requirements for backup sites are accessible/maintained

- *Supplies:* The following supply lists are maintained: list of critical supply items with all necessary information (e.g. stock number for ordering); list of vendors who provide supplies; and list/location of supplies needed for backup site processing

- *Transportation:* The following documents are maintained: the requirements for recovery operations/backup sites; the procedures for obtaining emergency transportation; and transportation procedures for staff in contingency situations

- *Specifications:* The contingency planning cover space (facilities) planning includes: the primary site requirements (layout of the facility); and backup site space available by site

- *Power and Environment:* Primary site and backup site requirements are maintained

- *Documentation:* On-site and off-site inventories are maintained; and the organization maintains a list/location of critical documentation needed for backup site processing

- *Test Plans:* Test scenarios are defined; a testing schedule is maintained and adhered to; and test results are logged with follow-up action monitored

Country	Regulatory agency	Source	Requirements
USA (continued)			• *Backup Operations and Recovery Actions:* The full backup and recovery have been defined to meet scenarios; all supporting plans are defined; the backup site can process the required volume; the backup site can provide sufficient processing time for as long as is necessary; a reasonable distance between primary and backup sites has been planned for; alternate site agreements are maintained to be consistent with backup and recovery strategies; contracts are up to date; and insurance coverage is consistent with recovery requirements
	NASD (National Association of Securities Dealers)	N/A	No published requirements on disaster recovery or business continuity plan, but members are examined for compliance with SEC regulations
	Foreign Corrupt Practices Act	N/A	Officers and directors of a corporation are legally responsible for the management of corporate assets, which include disaster recovery/business continuity
	Derivatives Policy Group (DPG)	Linkage Dbase DPG Dbase Credit Hub Entity Master FOSS BOSS	Procedures should be defined for general IT controls for applicable applications (e.g. disaster recovery plans)
JAPAN	Ministry of Finance Bank of Japan JSDA Securities Investment Trust Association	N/A	No information provided

ENGLAND	Bank of England	Bank of England Supervision and Surveillance (#S&S/1996/6 Part 3)	• In the event of a BoE Section 39 review, depending upon the scope set by the BoE, the lack of a formal disaster recovery plan would be reported as an exception • A formal plan that has never been tested would be reported as an exception • The guidance makes reference to the classification of the risk associated with IT in financial systems as "interruption—the components of electronic systems are vulnerable to interruption and failure; without adequate contingency arrangements, this can lead to serious operational difficulty and/or financial loss"
	Securities and Futures Authority (SFA)		Security of records: The firm must maintain procedures for the maintenance, security, privacy and preservation of records, working papers and documents of title belonging to the firm or others, so that they are reasonably safeguarded against loss, unauthorized access, alteration or destruction
	Securities and Investment Board (SIB)		Security of records: The institution must maintain procedures for the maintenance, security, privacy and preservation of records and documents of title belonging to customers, so that they are reasonably safeguarded against loss, unauthorized access, alteration or destruction
	Other		Accounting records have to be maintained for three years for a private company and six years for a public company; however, the VAT Act stipulates six years for any company registered for VAT. A disaster is not sufficient to avoid paying VAT, so records need to be maintained in all circumstances

Country	Regulatory agency	Source	Requirements
FRANCE	Not Indicated	No. 97-Cl regulation, article 14	• The bank ensures that its Information System (IS) control procedures adequately respond to the acceptable level of the IS risk set out. In case of a disaster, the IS control procedures should provide assurance that the BCP will guarantee the continuity of business operations
		IS Security Best Practices ("Livre Blanc")	• Management is responsible for the implementation and control of the BCP • The bank should determine how long the business can continue without its systems • The BCP should ensure the availability of critical data and processing • The BCP should be tested, and should address user procedures
GERMANY	German Federal Ministry of Finance	GAAP-CAAS C&L Deutsche Revision Bundesaufsich-tamt Pronounce-ment 10/92 FAMA Checklist	• The objective of data security measures is to avoid the risk of loss, destruction or theft of the backed-up programs and data • The risk of loss is to be eliminated by systematic documentation of the backed-up programs and data • The risk of the destruction of the data media is to be avoided by keeping them in a suitable place • Scheduled backups as well as ad hoc backups should be performed and stored in a different location. A systematic register of the backed-up programs and data files should be maintained • Backup retention locations should be safe from theft, fire, temperature, humidity or magnetic fields, etc. • Backups should be checked periodically • Information of relevance to the accounting must be capable of being presented in readable form at all times during the prescribed retention period • To enable the entity to comply with this requirement, it must ensure the availability of the hardware as well as the data and the software

- The data security concept must also provide for the safeguarding of the computer installations, e.g., hardware, data transmission lines
- The entity's data backup concept must be documented
- The entity's data security concept must be documented
- Generally, data performing voucher functions must be retained for six years, and data and other necessary records performing daybook or account function must be retained for ten years

Federal Banking Supervisory Authority

- There must be a written contingency plan which ensures backup trading systems are available in the event of equipment failure
- Precautions must be taken for possible faults in the software used and for unforeseen absences of staff
- Data processing procedures, documentation plans and contingency plans should be regularly reviewed
- The principles of cross-border remote data processing must be followed
- Firms must abide by the GAAP-CAAS (see FAMA) standards
- Data processing facilities should be adequately secured against breakdown
- Contingency plans should provide for suitable data backup and recovery facilities
- It must be possible to restore destroyed records within 24 hours. Under exceptional circumstances, such as total disaster, the 24 hour rule may be extended to 48 hours
- The computer site must be secured against unauthorized personnel through appropriate technical and constructional safeguards

Country	Regulatory agency	Source	Requirements
Germany (continued)			• There should be at least one off-site disaster recovery facility to guarantee continuing service • A written EDP concept must be available • There should be written procedures for the reconstruction of data files. These procedures should be tested to verify that reconstruction is possible • Data backup requirements for each application should be defined • Data backup files should be stored outside the computer center in fireproof cabinets and tested regularly • Alternate power supply and fire protection should be present • The firm should have an emergency plan defining alternate processing facilities for EDP applications • Continuity of operations must be ensured by use of an operating system which enables stored data and applications to be accessed in a reasonable timeframe • Completeness of data files should be controlled and this information should be kept up to date at all times • The retention period for each data file has to be defined • Arrangements should be made to ensure that data files can be processed throughout their retention period • The computer system should be regularly serviced by the manufacturer • Operating instructions should be available for each application • The computer room should be maintained at the required temperature and relative humidity

HONG KONG

Securities & Futures Commission

The general guidelines:

- An effective BCP appropriate to the size of the firm is implemented to ensure that the firm is protected from the risk of interruption to its business continuity. Key processes in this area include a business impact study, identification of likely scenarios involving interruptions, and documentation and regular testing of the firm's disaster recovery plan
- The firm has adequate insurance coverage for different types of exposures, including but not limited to fidelity insurance, and replacement of equipment and other business and data processing devices
- Registered dealers must retain accounting records for not less than six years. Contract notes received or issued by the dealer should be kept for not less than two years

Hong Kong Monetary Authority

- There should be contingency arrangements to mitigate the effect of the interruptions and to enable the business to continue operations in an orderly manner. Key control techniques and procedures suggested are:
  – A formal contingency plan should identify:
    - those operations that are critical to the continued survival of the business and which must therefore be continued
    - the key personnel who are needed to carry out those operations
    - premises, equipment (including EDP facilities) and files/documentation which are essential to carry out these operations
  – Responsibilities for formulating, updating, testing and implementing the contingency plan should be clearly defined

Country	Regulatory agency	Source	Requirements
Hong Kong (continued)			– Formal backup and/or off-site storage procedures should be arranged for all computer files and key documentation – Personnel should be provided with formal training on procedures to follow in case of disaster – Testing should be performed to ensure that the contingency plan is adequate to support the institution's most critical operations – Arrangements should be made with the hardware vendor or another company to provide backup hardware for data processing. In the case of purchased software, formal arrangements should be made to ensure that access to the master software can be made if the vendor ceases to trade – Backup and standby arrangements with outside parties should be confirmed and tested periodically • The adequacy of insurance against damage, disruption and the costs of recovery should be reviewed periodically
	Companies Ordinance		All companies should retain accounting records for at least seven years
ITALY	N/A	N/A	N/A
MEXICO	Commission Nacional Bancaria y Valores	N/A	No published requirements exist for DRPs or BCPs
AUSTRALIA	Bank of Australia		No published requirements on DRPs or BCPs
	Australian Security Commission		No published requirements on DRPs or BCPs
	Australia Stock Exchange		No published requirements on DRPs or BCPs

SINGAPORE	Monetary Authority of Singapore (MAS)	MAS guideline on Treasury and Financial Derivatives	Consistent with other systems plans, a written contingency plan for Treasury and Financial Derivative products should be in place. It should be tested periodically to ensure the applicability of the plan
CANADA	Office of the Superintendent of Financial Institutions (OSFI)		The OSFI looks for both a BCP and a DRP when performing audits. The BCP should arrange for business to proceed if any type of disaster should occur, and the DRP should arrange for data to be recovered if the primary supply is damaged. During a review, the OSFI ensures that these plans exist, and that they are successfully tested on a periodic basis (no specific time period was given to define "periodic")
	Canada Deposit Insurance Corp (CDIC)	CDIC 613–996–2081	The CDIC relies on the regulators (the OSFI and public accountants) to do this type of work. No additional reviews of DRPs and BCPs are performed by the CDIC
	Toronto Securities Exchange	Manager of Financial Compliance 416–943–6906	• Whether member firms make use of an external data center or an in-house computer system, a framework of controls must be established to ensure the accurate and continued processing of information for management and regulatory purposes. This framework includes the following requirements in regards to DRPs and BCPs: – In regards to data centers, management should be satisfied with the adequacy of internal controls within the data center, for areas such as: access to and confidentiality of data, back-up, supervision, and controls over operations and programs. This confidence may be provided by means of third party reviews, authorized discussions with the data center's auditors, or by having experienced internal staff or consultants meet with appropriate data center personnel

Country	Regulatory agency	Source	Requirements
Canada (continued)			– In regards to in-house computers, protection of facilities, programs and files, plans should be formulated and tested for the action to be taken in the event of a disaster that disrupts processing. This would include arrangements for alternate processing facilities and prioritizing the jobs to be run in the event of disrupted service. In addition, there should be adequate insurance coverage to cover hardware, software, business interruption, valuable records, alternate processing, and the cost of replacing data and programs
			– In regards to personal computers, hardware should be properly serviced, backed up, and safeguarded. Corporate policies on hardware selection and support may optimize these functions
			– In regards to telecommunications, there should be adequate procedures to control and recreate data lost during transmission
			– In general, it is recommended that an independent review of internal controls within the computer department be conducted by qualified internal or external auditors periodically (e.g. every two years)
	Ontario Securities Commission (OSC)		• Field reviews (audits) are done for Mutual Fund Dealers only; these started two years ago. During these reviews, the OSC looks at the internal controls and confirms that a DRP and a BCP exist. The OSC will ask questions until they feel comfortable with the plan. There are no published requirements for what the plans should contain. At some point in the future, these same reviews will occur for SROs (Self Regulatory Organizations). No start date has been announced
			• There are also Securities Commissions in Alberta, British Columbia, and Quebec. Ontario is the largest, and all of the other Commissions follow the Ontario guidelines

SWITZER-LAND	Federal Banking Commission (FBC)	• The regulators expect banks to implement good practices with respect to IT and contingency planning • Regulatory requirements are vague with respect to IT and contingency planning, which enables reasonable judgment by management – The requirement of having an "appropriate internal organization" for the banking license and the securities dealer license also covers disaster recovery and business continuity planning • Management should assess the impact that a loss of critical applications or computer facilities on key business functions, and mitigate the impact • There should be appropriate backup procedures for data and programs • The backups should be stored in a secure location • Backup and recovery procedures should be tested to ensure that they work when required
	Swiss Exchange	• Members are required immediately to inform the Swiss Exchange (Markets Division) of failures or material defects in their trading system as well as the restoration of normal processing. Members should also apply for permission to trade on a provisional basis • Trades should be reported to the Swiss Exchange as soon as possible after the end of an emergency situation, but at the latest before the opening of the following exchange day

Country	Regulatory agency	Source	Requirements
SWITZER-LAND (continued)	Swiss Financial Futures and Options Exchange (Soffex)		• Ordinance 6 of Soffex regulates the OTC emergency procedures for cases of system failures of the electronic derivatives exchange where GSB is a member. Notification to members is released through page 85, SOF11/12 of the Investdata System or by telephone alarm. Members will be informed of alternate procedures • In the event of a system breakdown, Soffex will determine if OTC trading will be released. Generally, if there are indications that trading can be resumed by the normal system within one hour of the system breakdown, OTC trading will normally not take place
GEORGE-TOWN CAYMAN ISLANDS	Cayman Islands Monetary Authority		No published requirements on DRPs or BCPs but member firms must submit audited financial statements within three months of fiscal year end

Table 1.2   BCP Phases and their components

Phase	Functions	Components
1. Project Foundation	Aligns management and sets expectations. This will eliminate much of the resistance you would otherwise encounter later on in the project when you try to set meeting appointments and schedule work sessions	Establishes the basis for a successful project. This includes establishing project expectations, obtaining appropriate commitments, selecting the appropriate participants, and establishing an efficient work plan
2. Business Assessment	Identifies both external and internal threats to the business. The information found in this phase will be the basis for the construction of strategies and the eventual BCP	Documents business unit critical processes and components and identifies existing and potential disaster-mitigating systems/procedures. This includes understanding the process flow of each business unit, determining the Recovery Time Objective, defining the business unit's critical resources, and identifying existing containment measures and exposures.
3. Strategy Selection	Employs a methodology to eliminate conditions that would put a company out of business if a disaster struck	Chooses an appropriate course of action or future undertaking to enhance the survivability of the critical components of the business. These include strategies to protect computer systems, communications, staff, facilities, equipment, office supplies, market share, and supplier continuity.
4. Plan Development	Puts together a choreographed sequence of actions that counteract or mitigate the effects of the threats or risks identified in the Business Assessment phase	Creates a document with the user that will re-establish the critical components of the business in the least possible time, and at the lowest cost to the business. The plan must be developed by the ultimate user using familiar terms and with references to sources of resource repair or replacement services. The plan should be easy to navigate and be understood by all participants of the recovery
5. Testing and Maintenance	Ensures that the BCP works and keeps it current	Evaluates the effectiveness of procedures and access to resources through disaster simulation and updating the BCP to reflect current conditions. Each procedure and resource must be evaluated to determine if it will be viable during a real disaster situation. The results of the evaluation will be used to update the BCP. Periodically, the plan will need to be reviewed and amended to reflect changes in staff, equipment, and procedures.

2   Project Foundation

INITIAL ASSESSMENT

Many times a company will want to understand where they are with regard to Business Continuity "Best Practices". By looking at a few key indicators, one can assess the viability of their organization's Business Continuity Planning program.

BCP EVALUATION

In order to evaluate the effectiveness and viability of an organization's BCP structure, you must gain an understanding of what has been put in place to mitigate disaster risks. As an overall indicator of the BCP structure, examine and evaluate the existing business continuity plan.

The first thing that you will want to determine is if a Business Continuity Plan currently exists. If a plan does not exist, then you have finished your evaluation. If the plan does exist, then there are further assessments that will be required to determine its effectiveness.

The following are techniques used to determine a plan's effectiveness:

- Determine if the plan has been revised within the last year.
- A plan should have team members that are assigned certain responsibilities during a recovery operation. Randomly select several team members and ask them if they know what their responsibilities are during a recovery situation.
- Select samplings of staff members listed in the plan and verify their home contact and emergency contact information (generally you will find this to be only 60% accurate).
- Determine if members of the senior management staff are included in the recovery plan (when real disasters occur, senior staff members tend to take control of

recovery efforts, regardless of what it says in the plan. It is best to include their roles in the plan initially).

- Call the vendors listed in the plan and determine if the service levels assumed in the plan could actually be delivered at the time of the call (you may find that the vendor was never contacted in the first place).
- Determine if backup schedules were the result of data criticality assessments or if they were the result of more arbitrary criteria.
- Assess whether all critical components of production have procedures, tasks, backup sources identified. Many plans address only a few key components of production such as Information Systems and Communications. What these plans fail to take into account is that an organization's ability to produce its product is dependent upon all its components of production being functional, not just a few.
- If a disaster occurs, determine if the plan identifies what should be retrieved from offsite storage? Who is authorized to retrieve materials? How is access to the stored materials to be accomplished?
- Find out if there is anyone in charge of maintaining the Business Continuity Plan.
- Perform a reality check to determine if team members realistically have the authority to carry out the recovery tasks assigned to them.
- Determine if critical production resources have been enumerated in the plan.
- Determine if those production resources have been associated with a vendor or other source that could provide a replacement resource item in the event of a disaster.
- Assess whether equipment specifications and layout configurations are adequately documented.
- Identify that the plan contains recovery team succession ordering.
- Determine if the plan has ever been tested.

Once you have gone through these determinations, you should have a fairly clear idea of what needs to be done to improve the business continuity planning structure of the organization.

PRE-ENGAGEMENT QUESTIONNAIRE

This questionnaire was designed for outside consultants to scope the amount of effort that will be required to complete an engagement. Internal project managers may also find this questionnaire beneficial for gathering information that will be used in project planning and budget requests.

You can use this BCP Evaluation Questionnaire to raise awareness of the shortcomings of the organization's BCP program. You can use the Pre-Engagement

Questionnaire to determine how much time and effort it will take to bring the present BCP program up to standard.

This Pre-engagement Questionnaire is the initial data mining operation of the engagement. It will identify the components of the organization, the number of interviews required, the assistance and cooperation available, and the expectations of the client.

Questions/requests	Comments
1. How many employees would fall within the scope of this engagement (generally, this is the number of employees working at the organization?)	This will give you an idea of the relative magnitude of the engagement and the number of consultants it will take. The number of employees listed should be compared with the organization's staff list.
2. Please provide an Organization Chart with names and positions.	The Organization Chart is a critical document. It will give you assurance that you have included all parts of the organization in your plan. It will also give you a hierarchy for conflict resolution.
3. Beneath the Chief Executive level of the Organization Chart is the second level of executives. Other than the second level executives, identify key staff members who should be interviewed in order to obtain an understanding of this organization's process flows.	Here you identify the number of staff that you will be interviewing. Also, you are letting the business know that you wish to interview the senior management of the organization and those that have highly technical skills such as the IT and Communications experts.
4. Do Business Continuity Documents/ Procedures currently exist (e.g. IPL procedures, evacuation procedures)? If yes, please specify:	If reasonable, these should be included in the BCP.
5. Will this project require us to meet with vendors whom your organization relies upon for various business processes or resources? If Yes, how many?	This will determine any additional interviews that will be required.
6. Will this project require us to meet with your major customers to determine their needs? If Yes, how many customers will we need to meet with?	This will determine any additional interviews that will be required.

7. Are *current* staff lists (which include an employee's home phone, address, and department) available?

This can be quite time consuming if you have to compile this list yourself. You will find that in most organizations the staff contact list is at least 40% inaccurate. If possible, have Human Resources verify the list's integrity before they give it to you. Also, try to get the data in a format that is compatible with your plan software.

8. Is a current vendor list, which includes the vendor's address (not PO Box), phone number, emergency contact, and explanation of service provided, available?

This list can also be quite time consuming to compile. You will find yourself copying information from roll-a-dex all over the organization. This list will be a critical component of the BCP.

9. Will a knowledgeable staff member be assigned to assist in this project?

If you are an outside consultant, you must have a knowledgeable staff member assisting you. Do not let the client assign a low-level clerk to the project as your assistant. This can kill your project.

10. Will adequate workspace be made available for work on this project?

It is important that you have adequate workspace and tools (printer, paper, telephone, data link, etc.) if you are to be efficient in producing the plan.

11. Is access to key individuals readily available, or must appointments be made to discuss BCP matters?

This has a tremendous bearing on the amount of time the engagement will take. The question sends the message that you expect your requests to be responded to promptly.

12. Would recovery team members (to be appointed later) be available for assisting in the development of BCPs?

If the answer is no, the plan will be less than effective. This question is a good indication of the overall commitment to the planning process by the organization.

13. What do you hope to achieve from a Business Impact Analysis?

What are the client's expectations? Many times the success or failure of a project is measured by whether or not expectations are met.

14. What are the main objectives you hope to receive from a BCP strategy activity?

Expectations again.

15. Is there a software preference for the development of the BCP?

You will want to use software with which you are familiar; but if the client insists, you may have to learn a new software.

These questions are the result of lessons learned from a number of consulting engagements that did not turn out as well as was expected. When the problems that were encountered were analyzed, it was found that setting up the engagement correctly would have avoided many painful situations later in the plan development process.

With all the information gained from the two questionnaires, you are now in a position to develop a Work Plan.

WORK PLAN

The Work Plan is a critical component of the plan development process. It is the guidepost that will allow you to complete the planning process in an efficient manner. The Work Plan should be developed prior to the proposal phase of the project. Once the steps have been determined, times can be assigned and summed, so that an estimate of the total hours required for completion can be determined. Based on the Pre-engagement Questionnaire, you will be able to assign a difficulty index to each step according to the amount of cooperation, commitment, and pre-existing documentation available from the client.

The following is an example of a Work Plan that has been used successfully in a number of BCP engagements:

SAMPLE WORK PLAN

WITH SENIOR EXECUTIVE OFFICER

1. Contact site senior executive officer and discuss what is to be accomplished and timeframes.
2. Get permission to proceed with engagement.
3. Have Senior Executive Officer designate a BCP Coordinator.
4. Update contact list with BCP Coordinator information.
5. Get recommendation on place to stay that is close to the target facility.
6. Set date of engagement commencement.

WITH PLAN COORDINATOR

1. Contact Coordinator and explain the program (the plan will be for ONE facility only. Explain the need for someone within the organization to train).
2. Tell Coordinator that you will need a Staff List (with department), Vendor List, and Organization Chart as soon as possible.
3. Tell BCP Coordinator that you need an IS inventory, equipment/communication schematics, and IS vendors. Get IS staff working on this immediately.
4. Determine the size of the IS staff and whether a mid-range and/or full-sized computer is on-site.

5. Determine if the facility is owned or leased. Determine if the lessor will take care of damages to the building.
6. Tell Coordinator that you will need: working space, a desk, a telephone, a PC monitor, A PRINTER WITH CABLE, and a keyboard. Ensure your PC is loaded with the correct print driver.
7. Tell the Coordinator that the morning you arrive there will be a 45-minute meeting with the Senior Executive Officer's direct reports. Indicate that you need an overhead projector or PC projector. Tell the Coordinator that you will meet with the direct reports for a 25 to 45-minute interview on the first day.
8. Determine if the organization has copy capabilities; otherwise locate a copy vendor for your printing requirements.

SOLIDIFICATION

1. Compile a pre-engagement package and send to the BCP Coordinator.
2. Assemble your team and conduct a briefing on the project.
3. Make travel arrangements.

ON-SITE PROJECT INITIATION

1. Request and receive existing plans.
2. Review plans.
3. Request and receive business function descriptions.
4. Review descriptions
5. Request and receive an annual report.
6. Review annual report.
7. Request and receive audit reports.
8. Review audit reports.
9. Request and receive insurance coverage.
10. Review insurance coverage with special attention to business interruption components.
11. Receive staff and vendor information.
12. Receive Organization Chart from site.
13. Call BCP Coordinator and confirm Organization Chart validity.
14. Create a new plan template (verify that there are no references to other plans).
15. Customize the plan template to accommodate new client.
16. Enter facility information.
17. Enter department information (if available)
18. Enter staff information.
19. Enter vendor information.
20. Enter storage information.
21. Enter regulators.
22. Create vendor maps.
23. Load customers if provided.
24. Request that site assembles one month's worth of supplies requisitions.
25. Create folders.
26. Modify Action Plan to reflect no mid-range computers (if appropriate).
27. Modify Action Plan to reflect ownership of building (if applicable).

28. Create Excel item input sheet.
29. Load staff titles into staff section.
30. Create risk assessments data sheets.
31. Update and print News Release template.
32. Verify the correctness of addresses and phone numbers of team members.
33. Print BIA data forms.
34. Create and print Item Input forms.
35. Print risk assessment sheet.
36. Print Emergency procedures.

TRAVEL PREPARATIONS

1. Determine the number of attendees at initial presentation.
2. Ensure overhead projector is available.
3. Call BCP Coordinator and ensure that materials and especially a printer will be available.
4. Make copies of initial presentation for attendees.
5. Travel to engagement site.
6. Tour facility and surrounding area.
7. Show up at facility one hour before presentation for set up.

RISK ASSESSMENT/BIA ANALYSIS

Organize
1. Meet with the plan manager. Assemble management team and present overview of project.
2. Identify reason for doing BCP.
3. Define project scope.
4. Determine timing criteria for plan creation.
5. Obtain management support in an initial meeting with the senior executive.
6. Determine staff to be interviewed.
7. Meet with plan coordinator and determine organizational structure. Prepare Organization Chart (if not previously prepared).
8. Determine desires of management for Progress Reporting (format, dates, i.e. weekly, daily, every other day, etc.).
9. Review the organization's strategic plans if available.
10. Prepare total Risk Assessment and Emergency Procedure Templates for review and modification.

RISK ASSESSMENT

1. Identify exposures that could impact operations.
2. List containment measures used to mitigate impact.
3. Identify and document backup methodology.
4. Obtain existing contracts and store offsite.
5. Identify and document change control procedures.
6. Obtain vital records schedule and retention records.
7. Obtain insurance coverage documents and store off-site.

8. Review all Risk Assessment information.
9. Prepare recommendations for enhanced containment.

EMERGENCY RESPONSE PROCEDURES

1. Collect all emergency and damage control procedures developed by the organization.
2. Review procedures.
3. Modify and enhance procedures as required.

BUSINESS INTERRUPTION ANALYSIS (BIA)

1. Meet with selected Business Unit Managers to complete BIA.
2. Review and document business process flows.
3. Complete item input sheet immediately following BIA.
4. If possible, get dollar values of outage at various durations.
5. Rank Critical Services and develop and distribute Critical Services document.
6. Prepare BIA report and present to management.

STRATEGIES

1. Prepare a cost/benefit analysis on engaging the services of a hot-site vendor (if appropriate).
2. Identify those services to be recovered initially.
3. Prepare recovery time line.
4. Prepare strategies list for Business Units.
5. Obtain Management concurrence.

BUSINESS CONTINUITY PLANNING DEVELOPMENT

1. Prepare and disseminate RFP for hot-site.
2. Help client select best hot-site.
3. Enter facilities data into plan.
4. Enter department information.
5. Load staff information.
6. Print Staff Report and pass out copies to Business Unit Managers for verification.
7. Enter duration information.
8. Contact critical vendors to determine their service commitment during a disaster situation (IT vendors, communications vendors, commercial real estate broker, insurance co., off-site storage facility).
9. Gather information and input data on vendors, customers, regulators, insurance company, and storage locations.
10. Print comparable reports and review.
11. Complete the resource item matrix for inclusion into the plan.
12. Obtain service commitments from critical internal dependencies.
13. Prepare procedures.
14. Prepare tasks.

15. With management, determine team composition.
16. Link procedures to teams.
17. Review procedures and tasks with teams.
18. Identify vendors linked to procedures.
19. Identify vendors linked to tasks.
20. Insert identified vendors into plan.
21. Link backup storage facilities to appropriate resource items.
22. Meet with management to determine the management succession order and team succession orders.
23. Input data to plan.
24. Print the plan.
25. Review the plan and make changes as necessary.
26. Distribute the edited plan to the appropriate members of management for review.
27. Make changes to the plan as necessary.
28. Print the final copy of the plan.

PREPARE APPENDICES

1. Load vendor information into mapping software.
2. Prepare Recovery Center procedure.
3. Prepare Public Relations News Release form.
4. Prepare any other appendices that might be required for the organization.
5. Create "print ready" proof copy of manual.
6. Have requisite number of copies of the Disaster Recovery Manual printed.

MAINTENANCE

1. Develop and communicate Guidelines for Plan Maintenance.
2. Develop change triggers.
3. Develop and communicate Schedule for Plan Maintenance to business units.

TRAINING

1. Prepare training materials and develop training presentation.
2. Train recovery team members in use of the plan.
3. Document attendees to training session.

TESTING

1. Develop objectives and scope.
2. Develop measurement criteria.
3. Prepare test script.
4. Conduct tests.
5. Modify BCP based upon results of test.
6. Document results.

The Work Plan is a tool that will be used daily to communicate to the assigned plan administrator (the staff member assigned to the project and the one who will maintain the plan) where we are in the process and what steps are coming next. The steps need not necessarily be followed in sequential order, but all steps must be accounted for by the end of the project. The Work Plan is an invaluable tool for keeping the project on track.

THE PROPOSAL

Now that the Pre-engagement Questionnaire and the Work Plan have been completed, from the data gathered and the Work Plan created you can assign hours to the tasks required for completion of the BCP. By converting hours into billable hours, you can determine a reasonable fee to charge the client. All the components are now available for the preparation of the Proposal. Below is a template proposal that is suited to the information that has been gathered.

A note of caution: ensure that the deliverables mentioned will in fact be delivered. One of the greatest hazards to a consulting firm is that of not being paid by the client. If the client reads the proposal at the end of the engagement and notes a promise that has not been met, it may be difficult to collect the consulting fees due.

SAMPLE PROPOSAL

DATE

NAME
TITLE
COMPANY
ADDRESS

Dear NAME:

Consulting Firm Name is pleased to have the opportunity to be of service to the **COMPANY** in your Business Continuity Planning efforts. We wish to partner with you to help protect your leadership position and brand name, and to assist you in your objective of maintaining uninterrupted customer service through unexpected disruptions in business operations. The purpose of this letter is to confirm our understanding of the scope and timing of professional services, to outline the project approach we will employ, and to confirm our understanding of the terms of our engagement to provide Business Continuity Planning services to the **CITY, STATE** facility.

OUR UNDERSTANDING

We understand that the **COMPANY** is committed to the development of a Business Continuity Plan that can be completed by the end of DATE. Accordingly, we will start no later than DATE and the **COMPANY** will limit the interview process to no more than **NUMBER** individuals (the exact number to be determined upon review of the Organization Chart) who will represent the total **COMPANY** functionality of the **ADDRESS** facility.

We understand that a strategy has not been developed, nor plans documented, to address a significant business interruption.

We understand that you will appoint a Business Continuity Planning project coordinator, who will be responsible for directing us to the information we need during the data gathering phase and coordinating key decision points throughout the project. Additionally, adequate workspace will be made available so that plan development can proceed on-site.

We understand that, to the extent possible, access to key individuals will be made available in order to accelerate the delivery of this important product.

PROJECT APPROACH

To achieve your objectives in a timely and cost effective manner, we will utilize our methodology and tools for Business Continuity Planning. Using this approach, your project will be divided into the following three distinct phases: Business Impact Analysis, Strategy Evaluation and Selection, and Business Continuity Plan Documentation.

Phase I: Business Impact Analysis

Consulting Firm Name will begin this project with a review of the **COMPANY**'s existing business continuity capabilities. This initial review will introduce selected **COMPANY** employees to the objectives and approach of the project while ensuring subsequent planning builds on all current work.

Using the review findings as a baseline, a Business Impact Analysis (BIA) will be created that will incorporate a consensus understanding of functions, resources, and recovery timeframes that are critical to the business continuity of the **COMPANY**. The BIA will:

- evaluate the risk to business process failures;
- identify critical and necessary business functions/processes and their resource dependencies;
- estimate the financial and operational impacts of disruption and the required recovery timeframe for these critical business functions; and,
- assess the effectiveness of existing risk reduction measures.

The project team will interview the **COMPANY**'s subject-matter experts. Most of these interviews will take approximately one hour. Given our understanding of your environment, we anticipate conducting as many as **NUMBER** interviews.

Consulting Firm Name will then collate, analyze, and compile all information obtained and provide the **COMPANY** with the following information contained in a BIA report which can be reviewed with appropriate members of the **COMPANY**'s management to ensure its adequacy for your purposes:

- financial impacts of disruption;

- operational impact of disruption;
- prioritized critical functions for business continuity;
- recovery time frames for critical functions;
- required resources (i.e. computer systems, vital records, telecommunications, and work areas) for business continuity.

Phase II: Strategy Selection

In this phase, **Consulting Firm Name** will recommend improvements to the **COMPANY** infrastructure to strengthen your ability to support the needs identified in the Business Impact Analysis. This phase is used to identify your recovery approach for existing processes, technology infrastructure, facilities, and the maximum acceptable recovery timeframe requirements. This phase will:

- identify a range of specific recovery strategies to address interruptions of production processes;
- identify the computing resources required to recover the various distributed processing environments; and
- document alternative recovery strategies within a Recovery Strategy Selection report to the **COMPANY**.

Phase III: Business Continuity Plan Documentation

In this phase, **Consulting Firm Name** will assist in the creation of the **COMPANY**'s Business Continuity Plan. The plan will address the following issues:

- emergency notification and disaster declaration procedures;
- recovery team procedures;
- facility and business restoration procedures;
- BCP testing and maintenance cycles; and,
- appendices for master contact lists, equipment inventories, connectivity schematics, etc.

Recovery teams will be formed and staffed by **COMPANY** employees and will provide the foundation of the Business Continuity Plan. These teams will manage or execute the recovery process.

Each team will consist of senior/skilled staff members who will be trained in the application of the BCP. **Consulting Firm Name** estimates that the **COMPANY** will require a number of recovery teams for its Business Continuity Plan. This number will be refined as the **COMPANY**'s recovery needs are confirmed.

Consulting Firm Name will review conceptual recovery procedures, compare them with the recovery needs identified in the Business Impact Analysis phase and, where practical, propose additional recovery measures for each recovery team. Recovery teams will work with **Consulting Firm Name** consultants to develop detailed recovery procedures for their plans. Jointly, we will create the detailed recovery procedures as dictated by the **COMPANY**'s recovery needs. These detailed procedures will be reviewed, modified, and incorporated into the final Business Continuity Plan document.

PROJECT DELIVERABLES

The project team will create deliverables during each project phase. These deliverables will initially be developed in draft form to allow for the **COMPANY**'s review and approval of assumptions, findings, conclusions, and recommended actions before the issuance of final reports. The timely review and approval of all deliverables, usually within 10 business days, is a key component in ensuring the project team's ability to achieve project time schedules. This approval process also ensures that the **COMPANY** assumes the ownership of the planning process. Our project deliverables are as follows:

Phase I: Business Impact Analysis

Consulting Firm Name will produce a Business Impact Analysis Report which will include:

- a prioritized listing of the **COMPANY**'s critical functions and the timeframe in which each should be recovered;
- estimated operational and financial impacts;
- minimum resource requirements to continue critical functions; and
- additional risk mitigation techniques.

Phase II: Strategy Evaluation and Selection

The primary deliverable from this phase will be a detailed strategy evaluation. We will present recovery strategy options for selection by senior management.

Using this information, you can make decisions about resource allocation for the **COMPANY**'s business continuity program. The current capabilities, as well as any alternate strategies implemented from the strategy selection, will then be incorporated into the business continuation planning of the next phase.

Phase III: Business Continuity Plan Documentation

- **Consulting Firm Name** will work closely with **COMPANY** staff to develop effective recovery procedures and tasks.
- Teams consisting of **COMPANY** management will be assembled and trained in recovery procedures.
- Critical data such as Staff Lists and Vendor lists will be gathered and assembled for use in the Plan.

All reports and deliverables relating to this project will be for the use of the **COMPANY** management and cannot be distributed to any third parties without the prior written consent of **Consulting Firm Name.**

Project Timing and Fees

To achieve the **COMPANY**'s objective of a documented Business Continuity Plan by the target dates, **Consulting Firm Name** proposes to perform these services commencing on Month Day, 2001 for an estimated fee of $___,000, excluding reasonable out-of-pocket expenses.

Phase	Description	Estimated Fees	Estimated Time
Phase I	Business Impact Analysis	$	# weeks
Phase II	Strategy Selection	$	# weeks
Phase III	BCP Documentation	$	# weeks
Total Professional Fees		$ __,000	

Our policy is to invoice 25% upon project initiation and progress bill monthly thereafter. Out-of-pocket and travel related expenses will be billed separately, at actual cost, as incurred.

The above fees are exclusive of the costs associated with the purchase and/or lease of any prevention or recovery resources or BCP documentation software identified during the project. It is the **COMPANY**'s responsibility to negotiate and/or contract for these products and services.

Our fees, like those of most professional firms, are based upon the time commitment of the assigned consultants. The professionals identified in this proposal represent a consulting team with experience in Business Continuity Planning.

If, during the course of our work, it appears that our fee will exceed our estimate or if the nature and scope of our work is significantly modified from this proposal, we will advise you immediately and we will not undertake additional work without prior approval.

OTHER MATTERS

Our proposed project team is described in Attachment 1. Other important matters are explained in Attachment 2 and are considered an integral part of this contract.

* * * * * * *

If you have any questions, please call **NAME** at **312-XXX-XXXX** or **NAME** at **312-XXX-XXXX**. If the services outlined herein are in accordance with your requirements and if the above terms are acceptable to you, please have one copy of this letter signed in the space provided below and return it to us.

Very truly yours,

Sent by:

The services and terms as set forth in this letter are agreed to.

By: _____
(Name of company official)

_____
(Title)

_____
(Date)

PROJECT TEAM

As part of the overall project organization, we recommend that at least one individual from the **COMPANY**'s management be assigned to the project team in addition to the business unit participants. **Consulting Firm Name** will assume overall responsibility for completion of the project. However, the use of a joint project team leader will result in the engagement being carried out in an efficient and effective manner. The use of the **COMPANY** staff will also provide a consistent contact for the project team, and will provide the continuity required to successfully complete the project. Our core project team will be composed of the following **Consulting Firm Name** staff.

NAME will serve as project Partner responsible for overall coordination of the engagement. **NAME** has directed a variety of BCP reviews for large, complex processing environments. He is co-leader of the Business Continuity Planning leadership for the firm. **NAME** will be responsible for ensuring the engagements meet the high quality standards set forth by **Consulting Firm Name** for consulting activities.

NAME 2, will serve as Project Manager. He has completed over **X** business continuity plans in his career. He has served as National Director of Disaster Recovery Planning for three companies. He will provide project management, consultation, and quality assurance to the project to ensure that deliverables are consistent with our standards and your expectations.

In addition to the core BCP team, **Consulting Firm Name** will assign other technical and industry specialists, as necessary, during the course of the project. We will also coordinate closely with **Consulting Firm Name** audit team and rely on their familiarity and knowledge of the **COMPANY**'s operations.

OTHER MATTERS

Management's responsibilities
The overall definition and scope of the work to be performed is the responsibility of management and management bears the full responsibility for the adequacy of the scope of the work for their purposes. Management is also responsible for making available to us, upon request, information relevant to the work to be performed and personnel to whom we may direct inquiries, as appropriate.

Release and indemnification
In no event shall **Consulting Firm Name** be liable to the **COMPANY**, whether a claim be in tort, contract or otherwise (a) for any amount in excess of the total professional fees paid by the **COMPANY** to **Consulting Firm Name** under this engagement letter; or (b) for any consequential, indirect, lost profit or similar damages relating to **Consulting Firm Name** services provided under this engagement letter, except to the extent finally determined to have resulted from the willful misconduct or fraudulent behavior of **Consulting Firm Name** relating to such services.

The **COMPANY** agrees to indemnify and hold harmless **Consulting Firm Name** and its personnel from any and all claims, liabilities, costs, and expenses relating to **Consulting Firm Name** services under this engagement letter, except to the extent finally determined to have resulted from the willful misconduct or fraudulent behavior of **Consulting Firm Name** relating to such services.

In the unlikely event that differences concerning our services or fees should arise that are not resolved by mutual agreement, we both recognize that a judicial resolution could be facilitated by waiving the right to a jury trial. Accordingly, management and we agree to waive any right to a trial by jury in any action, proceeding or counterclaim arising out of or relating to our services and fees for this engagement.

Other Matters
Any additional services that you may request and we agree to provide will be the subject of separate written agreements. This engagement letter reflects the entire agreement between us relating to the services covered by this letter. It replaces and supersedes any previous proposals, correspondence and understandings, whether written or oral. The agreements of the **COMPANY** and **Consulting Firm Name** contained in this engagement letter shall survive the completion or termination of this engagement.

All reports or other products of our work provided to the **COMPANY** will be restricted to use by the management and the Board of Directors of the **COMPANY** and cannot be distributed to any other parties without our prior written approval.

KICK-OFF MEETING

The client has accepted and signed the proposal that has been created. An agreed upon kick-off date has been set. The first major event that should take place is a kick-off meeting with the senior staff of the organization.

It is very important that the CEO and his/her director reports attend this meeting. You must make it clear to this group that the plan that will be written is the CEO's plan to get the organization operational again after a major disaster. If the plan is sanctioned only by a lower level of management (Chief Auditor, CIO, CFO), it will be difficult getting cooperation and information later on in the engagement.

During the kick-off meeting you must communicate the purpose of the engagement, namely to build a plan that will restore the organization's functionality as quickly and at the lowest cost possible after a disaster. There should be a description of the BCP and how it will work during a disaster situation. There should be an outline of the engagement scope and timeline.

The scope of the engagement must be set early on in this process. You must be vigilant in not allowing "scope creep", otherwise the engagement will consume many more hours than is in the budget. As a basic rule of thumb, one plan document can cover only one facility. There may be more than one plan for a single facility, but there cannot be a single plan for multiple facilities. Also, departments that are not housed in a facility should not be included as part of the continuity effort. If the client insists otherwise, consider preparing a separate plan for the exception department/facility. (*Hint*: redo the proposal at that point. The amount of work has just increased.)

There should be a description of the client's role in the engagement. You will want to ensure that a plan administrator is appointed at or before this meeting. This person will not only assist you in obtaining information and appointments, but will learn how the plan is put together (the administrator will be charged with the task of maintaining the plan once you have left).

An effective method of getting the senior management team in the correct frame of mind for this project is to present an overview of Business Continuity Planning. The following is the outline of a slide presentation that has been successfully used at a number of kick-off meetings.

PLANNING FOR BUSINESS CONTINUITY

Topics

Introduction to what will be covered in the presentation

- What is a disaster?
- Causes of a disaster condition
- The impact of today's disasters
- What is a BCP?
- BCP methodology

What is a Disaster?

A disaster is defined as a disruption of business operations that stops the organization from providing its critical services caused by the absence of critical resources:

- People and skill sets
- Facilities
- Communications
- Power
- Information access

Causes of a Disaster Condition

The point of this slide is to show that nearly one-third of all disasters are the result of loss of electricity.

- Natural disasters
  - Hurricanes
  - Tornadoes
  - Floods
  - Fires
- Utilities
  - Electricity
  - Water

- – Communications
- – Gas
- Human causes
  - – Strikes
  - – Sabotage
  - – Terrorism
  - – Viruses
- Equipment failures
  - – Information systems
  - – Telecommunications
  - – Production line
- Man-made
- Nuclear/biochemical
- Transportation
- Contamination

The Impact of Today's Disaster

- Financial perspective
- Human resources
- Increasing competition
- Increasing use of technology
- Liabilities

Financial Perspective

A disaster will impact on the financial health of an organization. Extra expenses and loss of cash flow cause an erosion of an organization's equity position. Time is the enemy.

- Normal operating expenses
  - – Salaries
  - – Rent
- Large extraordinary expenses
  - – Equipment replacement
  - – Temporary facility
- Revenue/cash flow stops
- Equity position weakened

Human Resources

Because organizations now employ fewer people, the loss of staff has a much greater impact than in the past:

- Downsizing
- Re-engineering
- Outsourcing

The loss of a staff member's productive services has a profound impact.

Increasing Competition in a Global Economy

Many organizations compete based on the level of service they provide. Those service levels will not be met after a disaster that may mean the loss of customers. Having a plan to return to business quickly can be key to keeping market share.

- Service levels
- Lost customers don't return

Increasing Use of Technology

Organizations have become dependent upon technology to the point where, if a disaster occurs, it would be difficult to operate in a manual mode:

- More information faster
- Fax
- Voice mail
- Local and wide area networks
- Imaging
- Decision support systems
- Technologically empowered CSR
- Internet access

Liabilities Associated with not Providing Products/Services

Management is responsible for ensuring the continuity of business and may suffer consequences if disaster recovery has not been adequately planned:

- Penalties associated with not meeting delivery schedules
- Shareholder/Board of directors' new expectations

What is a BCP?

Definition of a BCP:

- An integrated set of procedures and resource information that is used to recover from a disaster that has caused a disruption to business operations

Components of a good plan:
- It answers the questions:
  - Who?
  - What?
  - When?
  - Where?

Business Continuity Plan

What a BCP does:

- Upon the declaration of a disaster, it activates preapproved policies and authorities

- It restores the outflow of services with the least possible cost to the organization

BCP Management Concerns

General expectations of senior management for a BCP:
- Want a plan installed as quickly as possible while minimizing the cost and disruption to the organization
- Project planning
- Quality project leadership
- Training for staff
- Regulatory compliance
- A quality, workable plan
- A plan that can be easily updated

BCP Prerequisites for Success

- Management commitment.
- BCP
- Planning tools

Consultant tools that enhance the plan development process:
- Risk assessment
- Business impact analysis method
- Planning software
- Emergency procedures

BCP Methodology

Risk assessment

Evaluation of the local environment:
- Evaluates risk present in the local environment
- Identifies measures taken to mitigate the risk
- Identifies measures that need to be taken
- Impacts the creation of the action plan

Business Impact Analysis

Understanding the critical nature of each business function:
- Identifies which services are essential
- Ranks services to avoid inter-organizational disputes
- Establishes recovery time objectives (RTO)
- Identifies loss impact at various durations
  - Income
  - Customer service

- Operating expenses
- Fines and penalties
- Staff productivity
- Service to other business units

Strategies

Strategy considerations:
- Customer contact
- Customer service
- Customer perception
- Include every part of organization, not just the computer room
- Customer/vendor knowledge
- Determine and plan for local authorities service levels

Examples of various strategies to consider:
- Facilities
- Hot-site
- Acquire replacement building
- Staff
- Layoffs
- Daycare/housing
- Who performs recovery
- Other resources
- Minimal equipment
- Electricity
- Communications
- Functionality
- Vendor selection

Emergency Procedures

Procedures to be used immediately after a disaster:
- Prevent a situation from becoming a disaster
- Human safety
- Action steps
- Damage control
- Plan around the limitations of the local authorities
- Integrate with disaster recovery plan

Plan Development

Brief explanation of how the plan is put together:
- Modify proven procedures
- Management feedback and revisions
- Resource linkages

Overview of Key Concepts

Explanation of the logic of the BCP:

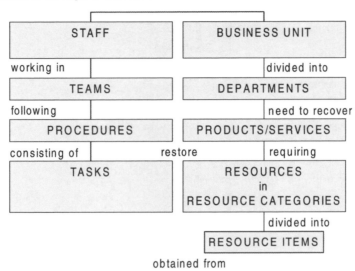

Plan Content

Description of how the plan will be organized:
- Instructions
- Action plan
- Procedures
- Resources
- Responsible teams
- Vendors
- Inventories
- Plan locations
- Succession lists
- Appendices
- Action plan expansions
- Regulatory requirements
- Maps, news release, etc.

And Finally

Review the plan for consistency, train teams in how to use the plan, types of testing available, and how to maintain the plan:

- Plan review
- Staff training
- Plan testing
  - Plan familiarization
  - Simulation
  - Component testing
  - Full business test
- Plan maintenance

A presentation such as this will take the client from generalities about BCP down to the specifics of what is going to be done during the engagement. It is very effective in getting the client to become mentally involved in the process. By the time you finish this book, you should be able to give a presentation similar to this during your kick-off meeting.

POLICY STATEMENT

Once you have obtained consensus from senior management on the value of Business Continuity Planning it is beneficial to transmit that message to the organization. This can best be accomplished through the construction of a corporate BCP policy statement. The following is a policy statement template that can be used in assisting the senior management of the organization to develop a BCP policy statement.

XYZ CORPORATION
POLICY ON DISASTER RECOVERY/BUSINESS CONTINUITY

Purpose

This policy statement defines X Y Z CORPORATION'S (X Y Z's) policy on assessing risks associated with threats to business continuity and for devising appropriate BCPs.

Business impact analysis is the process of evaluating the potential impact of a major interruption to business activity at a specific business location. Based on the level of risk, an essential aspect of any operation is to prepare a BCP that provides for the continuity of business in an emergency situation. Each business unit is responsible for compliance with any other applicable local or state regulations not mentioned in the policy.

This policy defines a framework for:

- Assessing a business unit's exposure to continuity risk and determining the necessity for a BCP.
- Developing an appropriate and cost-effective BCP that will ensure the continuity of business in emergency situations.

Requirements for business impact analysis and business continuity planning are auditable and require compliance.

Scope

This policy applies to all business units and all controlled subsidiaries and affiliates worldwide within X Y Z.

A business unit is defined as one or more organizations within X Y Z that provide products or service to customers or other business units within X Y Z. A business unit may be composed of one or more operating locations. For the purpose of this policy, the business unit management responsible for each operation location will determine risk.

Based upon the level of assessed risk, a business unit may or may not be required to develop a BCP. When a BCP is required, the plan will not be restricted to computer operations. Procedures for the continuity of business apply to all service functions, whether or not they are supported by computer systems.

The BCP will develop action plans for the reactivation of all vital components of a service. Additionally, the BCP will include provisions for the loss of service of external agents upon which X Y Z is critically dependent.

Compliance

The business impact analysis and BCP must be updated annually and within 30 days of any major operational or system change that has a material effect on the contingency strategy of a given operation. The assessment need not be completely redone every year; where the risks are essentially unchanged a confirmation of the adequacy of the existing assessment will suffice.

According to this policy, the BCP must be continually reviewed to ensure the continuity of business in the event of emergency or crisis. A formal review for relevance and adequacy must be conducted semi-annually and results documented by line management. The plan must then be updated to keep it current.

For high-risk business units or locations, the plan must be tested annually or within 30 days of major changes to the operation environment when such changes invalidate the results of previous tests.

Emergency Conditions

It is the policy of X Y Z Corporation to provide for continuity of business in the event of emergency conditions and other crises. The following business disruptions must be considered:

- Natural disasters (e.g. fire, floods, earthquakes)
- Inclement weather (e.g. hurricanes, tornadoes, snowstorms)
- Utilities failures (e.g. electricity, telephone, water, communications, heating, air conditioning)
- Strikes or similar job actions

- Transportation strikes or breakdowns
- Civil unrest, intrusions, sabotage, terrorism, riot, bombs
- Neighboring hazards (e.g. nearby chemical/explosive operations, airports, high crime areas, toxic spills and contamination, nuclear disasters)
- Loss of data processing support
- War

Business Continuity Planning

A BCP provides for continuity of business in instances where threats, including those to internal control and physical security, may become successful in causing major damage and/or disruption to the organization's critical business operations or services.

All business operations and services will develop, maintain, and test a BCP so that critical functions, information assets, or processing capability can be recovered after the discovery of a loss or failure. The BCP will be based on the criticality of the operation or service as specified in the business impact analysis and concurred with by the Audit Division.

Responsibilities of Management

Business management will:

- Assess the criticality of each business operation and associated information processing service and determine the risk to the business of their delay or loss
- Complete a business impact analysis
- Contain and/or manage the risks in accordance with this policy
- Prepare and keep current BCPs commensurate with the level of risk
- Ensure that the BCPs are tested on schedule

The Audit Division is responsible for concurring that:

- Risks appear to be properly dimensioned
- Containment measures selected appear adequate
- BCPs appear adequate and commensurate with risk
- Testing has been successfully conducted at least once annually
- The plans are being maintained

Major elements of a BCP

The following major elements must be addressed in a BCP so that the continuity of business operations is assured:

General Elements

- Management backup and succession procedures
- Procedures for a smooth and effective implementation of the BCP to cover emergency conditions
- Assessment of the impact of emergency conditions and the loss of information processing and tele/data communications support on the critical functions of the corporation

- Employment of methods to reduce, eliminate, and/or insure against such risk and/or impact to a prudent level
- Establishment of and familiarity with an emergency voice and data communications plan
- Facilities and manpower requirements
- Program for cross-training staff members to provide flexibility of assignment in times of emergency
- Semi-annual review and update of the BCP to assure its relevance and adequacy
- Periodic testing, at least annually, of BCPs in order to demonstrate and document their continued efficacy

Information Services and Data/Voice Communications Element

- Information backup, recovery and restoration procedures, including a vital records storage program
- Provisions for securing off-site backup of critical data files, software, documentation, forms and supplies
- Alternate means of processing work and maintaining services electronically and/or manually, including provision for needed off-site hardware, premises, and any other resource items
- Equipment backup and repair
- Electrical power backup
- Communications backup including provisions for voice and data services

The Board of Directors of X Y Z Corporation will annually review and approve management's assessment of how emergency conditions or a loss of information services support would impact operations and the methods to be employed to reduce or eliminate such risk and/or impact. The annual review and approval will be noted in the minutes of X Y Z Corporation Board of Directors.

Having the policy statement approved and adopted by the executive levels of the organization will facilitate your ability to complete the remainder of the planning project.

DATA REQUESTS

After the organization's staff is aware that a BCP is going to be built, you should begin to amass the data that will give your plan substance. The following is the "shopping list" that should be sent out prior to the official kick-off of the actual plan creation:

1. **Staff listing.** I have included a sample of the data items that I will need for the detail staff listing. As you can see, I will need employees' names, title, home

address and phone number, and an emergency contact number (mobile phone or beeper) if available. If you get this list from Personnel, you may have to check the currency of the data. It would be great if I could get this data in an Excel or Access format (saves on re-keying the data).

2. **Vendor requirements**. The well-written plan will have vendors for each of vital resources. If you identify these vendors and include them in the Vendor Listing, it would be a big help.

3. **Vendor listing.** Like the staff list, it is important to have vendor information that includes address (not PO box), phone number, emergency contact number, contact name, and the service or product that this vendor provides. In the event of an emergency it may be necessary to drive to one or more of these vendors to obtain specific goods or services. I would also like these in an Excel or Access format if possible.

4. **Storage locations.** The address, telephone number, contact name, and the items stored at off-site storage facilities.

5. **Customers**. Key customers that we would contact in the event that we had a major disaster and would be out of operation for several days.

6. **Computer system/communications configurations.** This information is important if we are trying to get exact replacements for our existing computer and communications systems.

7. **Supplies.** In order that we do not have to ask managers to estimate the number of paper clips and pens used in a typical month, we need to get the *Supplies Invoice* for a typical month. This will be used to stock a new facility, if required.

8. **Existing BCPs or emergency procedures.** We need these so that the new procedures will be consistent with those that exist currently.

The following are examples of each of the requested items. Examples are provided as a means of suggesting the preferred format.

DETAILED STAFF LISTING

Sandy **Acree** 7420 Wynne Place #4	Final Production Mgr. Richie FL 33133 555–467–0621	New Business
Norm **Andrews** 23807 Mountain Meadow	POS Representative Bright FL 33133 555–637–5763	POS
Paul **Aniskovich** 3435 Golden Ave. #1003	President & CEO Richie FL 33133 555–321–9877	Executive
Peter **Aniskovich** 9220 Deercross Pkwy #2A	Assoc. Chief Underwriter Richie FL 33133 555–791–4226	Underwriting
Jack **Ballenger** 4 Davenport Rd.	Remote Underwriter Richie FL 02670 555–394–4930	Underwriting

Donna **Barrett**	Sr. UW Requir. Coord.	New Business
8 Highland Meadows #4	Richie FL 33133 555–781–3266	
Joel **Beasley**	Co-Op	New Business
3283 Lunsford Dr	Richie FL 33133 555–734–7652	
Don **Behne**	Asst. V.P., & Controller	Accounting
7047 Ashwood Knolls	Richie FL 33133 555–868–7248	
Bill **Brielmaier**	Staff Accountant	Accounting
3970 Delmar Ave	Richie FL 33133 555–481–8424	

VENDOR REQUIREMENTS FOR KEY RESOURCE ITEMS

Voice Lines

Telephone Hand Sets

Backup Tape Storage Location Custodian

Data Communications Lines Installation

Microcomputer Equipment

Backup Facility

Window Repair

Roof Repair

Water Removal

Electrical Repair

Emergency Electric Power

Mud Removal

Emergency Closing Rooms

Furniture/Equipment Movers

Document/Electronic Media Restoration

Staff Replacement

Office Furniture

Office Equipment

Stationery & Supplies

Forms

DETAIL VENDOR LISTING

3Com Corporation 5400 Bayfront Plaza	**PHONE** **FAX**	3COM Superstack II Hub Switch 1000 (2), 3000TX, network cards.
AcuPrint, Inc 6359 Paceo Del Lago, Suite 400, Carlsbad, Ca 92009	**PHONE** (760) 929–4808 **FAX** (760) 929–4822	MICR toner cartridges for check printing
Aetna—AET 151 Farmington Avenue TSA-1	**PHONE** (800) 238–6252 **FAX**	AETNA—AET
Airborne Express POB 662, Seattle, WA 98111	**PHONE** (800) 722–0081 **FAX**	Freight and Express Mail
Alling and Cory POB 3037 Harisburg, PA 17105	**PHONE** (717) 761–6064 **FAX**	Printing supplies/Paper supplies
American Bankers Insurance P.O. Box 389	**PHONE** (215) 230–0850 **FAX**	American Bankers Insurance
American Heritage Life 1776 American Heritage Life Drive	**PHONE** (904) 992–1776 **FAX**	American Heritage Life Insurance
American Life & Casualty 2200 Ben. Franklin Pkwy # 105 N	**PHONE** (800) 422–0557 **FAX**	American Life & Casualty Company
American Mayflower Life of New York P.O. Box 3045 New York	**PHONE** (888) 265–5433 **FAX**	American Mayflower Life of New York

Storage Location Detail Report

National Underground Storage

Address:

Santa Ana, Texas 24278

Phone Number: (555) 794–8474   **Emergency Phone:**

Fax:

Contact Name: Gill Trapp   **Contact Title:**

Item: IT backup tapes   **Media:** Tapes

On-site Backup: Full backups weekly, with nightly incrementals. Tapes: 124 4 mm, 96 8 mm, 48 CompaqIII, 72 Compaq IV

Off-site Backup: Previous week's full backup goes to NUS after the weekly backup. Tapes: 2 4 mm, 4 8 mm, 6 CompaqIII, 8 CompaqIIIXT, 10 Compaq IV

Backup Frequency: Nightly

CUSTOMER LIST

Benefit Services/CNA Travelers	Reisterstown, FL 31136	Insurance Carrier
111 Business Center Drive	(410) 526–2222	
Blue Cross/Blue Shield	Newark, FL 33133	Insurance Carrier
7 Penn Plaza East PP04A	(305) 466–2222	
BYSIS Insurance Services	Miami, Fl 33133	Insurance Carrier
4200 Crums Mill Road	1–800–692–2222	

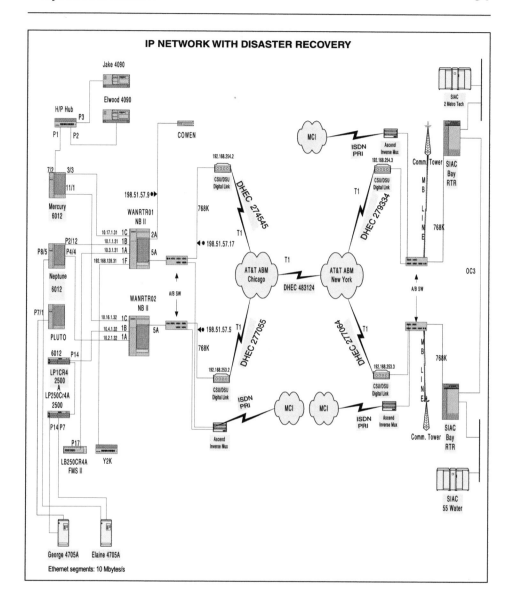

IP NETWORK WITH DISASTER RECOVERY

SUPPLIES

The following is a typical month's worth of office supplies:

QTY	DESCRIPTION	CATALOG #	U/M		
	ENVELOPES—NON-PRINTED				
	10 × 13 Brown Clasp Envelopes	SPR-08897	BX		
	Large Inter-office Envelopes	QUA-63561	BX		
	Small Inter-office Envelopes	QUA-63362	BX		
	Mini Diskette Mailers, 25/ctn	AVE-18274	EA		
	FILING SUPPLIES				
10	ACCO Binder, yellow	ACC-25070	EA		
	File Folders, ⅓ cut	SPR-SP111⅓	BX		
	File Folders, ⅕ cut	SPR-SP111⅕	BX		
	File Folders, ⅓ cut, 2nd Pos	SMD-153L-2	BX		
	Hanging File Folders	SPR-SP52⅓	BX		
	Hanging File Folders, ⅓ cut (CF only)	ESS-4152-⅓	BX		
	Label Holder, 1-⅛ × 3-½"	ACC-18802	PK		
	Label Holder, 2 × 3-½"	ACC-18804	PK		
5	Redrope Expanding Folder, 3-½"	SMD-1524E	EA		
	Redrope Expanding Folder, 5-¼"	SMD-1534GB	EA		
6	Ring Indexes, Clear 5-tab	SPR-01812	ST		
	Vinyl Sheet Protectors	AVE-74106	BX		
	LABELS				
	Laser Label	AVE-5162	BX		
	Laser Label	AVE-5266	BX		
	Laser Label	AVE-5160	BX		
	Laser Label, Shipping	MAC-ML0600	BX		
	MAGNETIC MEDIA				
	BASF, 3.5" DS/HD Diskettes, Formatted	BAS-54040	BX		
	RIBBONS				
	Wheelwriter 5 & 6 Typewriter Ribbon	LEX-1380999	EA		
	Wheelwriter 5 & 6 Typewriter Correction Tape	LEX-1337765	EA		

QTY	DESCRIPTION	CATALOG #	U/M		
	STAMPS				
	Ink Tubes for Daters, Blue, 5/pk	SHA-22013	PK		
	Ink Tubes for Daters, Red, 5/pk.	SHA-22011	PK		
	Self inking "Air Mail" x-stamper	SHA-1001	EA		
1	Staples, Standard	SPR-HB210	BX		
	Staples, Heavy Duty, ⅜"	SWI-35318	BX		
1	Glue Stick, .74 oz.	MCO-99649	EA		
	PAPER				
	Narrow Ruled Tablet	SPR-5084SP	DZ		
	Post-it Cover-up Tape	MMM-658	EA		
2	Post-it, 1-½ × 2, yellow, 12/pk.	MMM-6539-YW	DZ		
	Post-it, 2 × 3, yellow	MMM-6569-YW	PD		
5	Post-it, 3 × 3, yellow	MMM-6549-YW	PD		
3	Post-it, 3 × 5, yellow	MMM-6559-YW	PD		
	Correction tape, 1-line	MAC-MCR-16	RL		
	Strip Tab Insert, 5p.	KLF-6131	BX		
	Quadrille Pads, 10/bx	AMP-22000	EA		
1	Adding Machine Rolls, 2-¼	SPR-21500	EA		
	Cross-Section Pad	AMP-22020	EA		
	Filler Paper, 3-hole	AMP-26020	C		
	While U Were Out Pads	MMM-7664-4	DZ		
	Wide-Ruled Tablet	SPR-5082SP	DZ		
	Routing Request Notes, 12/pk.	MMM-7664-4	DZ		
5	Gregg Shorthand Notebooks	AMP-25-270	EA		
	Legal-Ruled Pad, Legal Size	SPR-2014	DZ		
2	Legal-Ruled Pad, Junior Size, 5 × 8	SPR-2058	DZ		
	Ultra Fine Flair, Black	PAP-833-01	EA		
	Ultra Fine Flair, Blue	PAP-831-01	EA		
	Ultra Fine Flair, Green	PAP-834-01	EA		
	Ultra Fine Flair, Red	PAP-832-01	EA		

QTY	DESCRIPTION	CATALOG #	U/M		
	Flair w/point guard/Black	PAP-84301	EA		
	Flair w/point guard/Red	PAP-84201	EA		
	DESK SETUP SUPPLIES				
	Wire Step File	FEL-72604	EA		
	Stack Tray, Letter	RUB-160003	EA		
	WRITING INSTRUMENTS				
1	.05 mm Lead Refill	PEN-C505HB	TB		
1	.07 mm Lead Refill	PEN-50HB	TB		
	Bic Accountant Fine Black Pen	BIC-AF11BK	DZ		
	Bic Accountant Fine Blue Pen	BIC-AF11BE	DZ		
	Bic Accountant Fine Red Pen	BIC-AF11RD	DZ		
2	Papermate Med Stick Black Pen	PAP-333-11	DZ		
25	Papermate Med Stick Blue Pen	PAP-331-11	DZ		
	Papermate Med Stick Red Pen	PAP-332-11	DZ		
	Pencils, #2	SPR-505-2	DZ		
	Correction Fluid, Pen & Ink	PAP-24711	EA		
	Correction Fluid, Just for Copies	PAP-710-01	EA		
5	Correction Fluid, FOREVERY, WE	BIC-WOC-12WE	EA		
1	Dry Erase, 4-color set	DIX-92040	ST		
	Dry Erase Broad Tip, Black	SAN-83001	EA		
	Eraser	QRT-804526	EA		
3	Highlighter, Blue	BIC-BL11BE	EA		
3	Highlighter, Green	BIC-BL11GN	EA		
5	Highlighter, Yellow	BIC-BL11YW	EA		
3	Highlighter, Pink	BIC-BL11PK	EA		
	Pencil Cap Erasers	FAB-70569	PK		
	Pentel Eraser Refills, 3/tb.	PEN-Z2-1	TB		
	PAPER FAST				
	Staple Remover	LEO-050	EA		

QTY	DESCRIPTION	CATALOG #	U/M		
	810 Magic Mending Tape, ¾" × 1296	MMM-6200-34-1296	RL		
	811 Scotch Cello Tape, ¾" Removable	MMM-811-34-1296	RL		
2	600 Scotch Cello Tape	MMM-5910341296	RL		
1	Binder Clips, Large	SPR-87010	DZ		
3	Binder Clips, Medium	SPR-87005	DZ		
5	Binder Clips, Small	SPR-87002	DZ		
3	Paper Clips, Small	SPR-85001	CN		
1	Paper Clips, Jumbo, SMTH, 1C	SPR-85009	C		
	Rubber Bands, #33, 1 lb./bx	SPR-331LB	BX		
	Rubber Bands, #117B, 1 LB	SPR-1171LB	BX		
1	Acco Two-Piece Fastener, 2", 50/bx.	ACC-70022	BX		
	DESK SETUP SUPPLIES				
	Scissors, Economy, STR, 7"	ACM-125-7	PR		
	Tape Dispenser, Desk, Black	MMM-C38-BK	EA		
	Stapler, Black	SWI-40701	EA		
	Post-it Note Tray, 3 × 5, Black	MMM-C4235	EA		
	Copyholder Stand, Black	FEL-21106	EA		
	Wastebasket, Plastic, 15H, BGE	RUB-295600BGE	EA		
	Board, Dryerase, 48 × 36	QRT-S534	EA		
	Large Add-A-File, Smoke	RUB-1711003	ST		
	Small Bookends, Tan, 5"	SPR-BS240	PR		
	Large Bookends, Tan, 9"	SPR-BS440	PR		
	Paper Punch, 3-Hole, Black	SPR-00786	EA		
	Desk Drawer Organizer	ROG-45721	EA		
	Ruler, Wooden, 12", single edge	ACM-R501B12	EA		
	Hanging Hot File, 4 pocket	RUB-1668003	ST		
	Calendar, Flip Style w/base	KEI-E17-00	EA		
	Calendar, Flip Style Refill	KEI-E017-50	EA		
	Monthly Minder w/holder	KEI-SK8-00	EA		
	Monthly Minder Refill	KEI-SK8-50	EA		

QTY	DESCRIPTION	CATALOG #	U/M		
	Desk Pad Calendar, 22 × 17	KEI-SK24-00	EA		
	Pocket Calendar	KEI-SK-48-00	EA		
	Pentel Mechanical Pencil, .05mm	PEN-P205A	EA		
	Pentel Mechanical Pencil, .07 mm	PEN-P207C	EA		
	Pushpins, Plastic, Clear	SPR-81002	PK		
	Blue Squeeze Bottle	SPR-01487	EA		
	Ballpoint Pen Refills, Blue	ESP-S01	EA		
	Wrist Rest, Padded	CCP-94300	EA		
	Mouse Pad	FEL-58016	EA		

Often, these lists will be difficult to get, which is why it is important to make the request for them early and to monitor their completion and return throughout the project.

3 Business Assessment

The Business Assessment is divided into two components, Risk Assessment and Business Impact Analysis (BIA). Risk Assessment is designed to evaluate existing exposures from the organization's environment, whereas the BIA assesses potential loss that could be caused by a disaster.

RISK ASSESSMENT

Risk Assessment is an evaluation of the exposures present in an organization's external and internal environment. It identifies whether or not the facility housing the organization is susceptible to floods, hurricanes, tornadoes, HVAC failure, sabotage, etc. It then documents what mitigating steps have been taken to address these threats. Table 3.1 is a form that can be used to step you through each potential exposure. For each threat that is relevant, you should determine the preventive measures that are in place. By crossing off those measures that do not exist, you are left with a report of which mitigating measures are present in the organization. By examining the preventive measures that were crossed off, you can compile a list of recommendations for improvement.

BUSINESS IMPACT ANALYSIS (BIA)

A BIA is an assessment of an organization's business functions to develop an understanding of their criticality, recovery time objectives, and resource needs.

By going through a Business Impact Analysis, the organization will gain a common understanding of functions that are critical to its survival. It will enable the client to achieve more effective planning at a lower cost by focusing on essential corporate functions.

Table 3.1 Risk assessment worksheet

Threats	Consequences	Preventive measures
Severe Storms/ Hurricanes	• Can be accompanied by flooding, loss of utilities, structural damage, falling trees, etc. • Use of damaged equipment and records can lead to processing errors. • Can delay or prevent staff from reaching work. • Loss of physical access. • Cessation of business activities.	• The building is constructed to meet local and state building codes. • Plastic bags are available to protect documents and magnetic media. • Vital records and all data processing facilities are located above the first floor that protects them from flooding. • Cross-training is an on-going process. This guards against the loss of staff. • There is a multitude of motels in the area to provide temporary housing in case staff members have to remain close to work. • Windows can be easily covered with hurricane shutters. • Doors are fortified to prevent wind intrusion. • Roofs are securely fastened to the structure with hurricane straps. • There is a "safe room" within the facility. • Critical equipment is protected from building collapse and flying debris. • Storm preparation procedures have been established.
Fire/Explosion	• Can be the direct or indirect result of other natural disasters. • Can be caused by equipment failure, accident or sabotage. • Water and other damage can occur while fighting the fire. • Facilities can be destroyed or rendered unusable for an extended period. • Processing can be interrupted for an extended period. • Assets and vital records can be lost. • The business can be interrupted with resulting penalty interest and legal claims. • Loss of voice/data communications • Personnel injuries and/or deaths	• Fire/smoke detection and alarm systems are in place and are monitored on a continual basis. • Air ducts are equipped with power dampers to prevent/minimize smoke migration. • The computer room is configured to minimize the extent of fire damage (kill switches are on sprinklers so that power in the computer room goes off before water sprays). • Fire suppression systems in the form of fire extinguishers and sprinkler systems are found throughout the building on every floor. • Fire extinguishers are found near the exits of the computer room. • Employees are trained in fire-fighting equipment. • Employees are trained in emergency shut down procedures. • Employees are trained in reporting emergencies. • Employees are trained in evacuation procedures.

- Exit routes are posted and exit route signs are found throughout the building.
- Smoking is restricted to safe designated areas.
- Diesel fire pump and reliable water source available for fighting fires.
- Fire separations are provided where needed for vertical and horizontal cutoffs.
- Preventive maintenance is performed on potentially hazardous equipment.
- Blank paper stock is not permitted in the computer room except for the current day's requirement.
- Flammable/combustible liquids and gases/fuels are stored and handled in an approved manner.
- Firewalls have been installed to restrict the spread and impact of a fire.
- Printed materials and garbage are removed from the computer room on a regular basis.
- Combustible materials are stored in areas suited for that function.
- All combusters are maintained and have been safety inspected.
- All pressure vessels are maintained and have been safety inspected.
- Emergency alarms are transmitted to a place of constant attendance.
- Dry vegetation that could contribute to a fire is kept cut.
- There are procedures for fire department notification.
- The fire department has toured and has a diagram of the facility.
- The area under the raised floor is cleaned regularly.
- The building is constructed to reduce the potential for fire.
- The building is located away from potential hazards that could restrict access of the fire department.
- A FM200 fire suppression system has been installed in the computer room.
- There are no housekeeping related hazards.
- There are crash bars on emergency exit doors.
- Emergency exits/routes/lighting/alarms are checked and tested regularly.
- Locks in the computer room release when the fire alarm sounds.

Threats	Consequences	Preventive measures
		• Closets and unused areas are equipped with fire/smoke detection and alarm systems. • Tile lifters are available in raised floor environments to investigate alarm conditions and fire suppression. • Macros are available for the rapid shutdown of systems. • Backup tapes and the System Administrator's Manual can be assembled and carried off site in a very rapid manner. • Backup copies of vital magnetic media are securely stored off-site. • Backup copies of vital paper records are securely stored off-site or maintained in a fireproof environment.
Internal Electrical Power	• Transients caused by variations in building load can occur. • Failure of power distribution system can occur. • Can cause processing failures. • Can cause equipment damage and excessive downtime.	• Emergency lights have been installed. • In the event of a loss of commercial electricity, electric power can be maintained through emergency generators located at the facility. • The power from the emergency generator can maintain the organization's vital functions. • Circuits are protected by circuit breakers. • Cords/wiring are kept in good shape. • Uninterrupted power source equipment is used throughout the building. • The uninterrupted power supply (UPS) system is monitored around the clock. • Exit lights are clearly visible. • Procedures are in place to recover from a power failure. • Preventive maintenance of emergency power equipment is routinely conducted. • Power distribution systems are protected from hazards such as fire, water, accident, and sabotage. • Hazards of overcurrent have been assessed using single line diagrams, equipment data and utility system data.

Commercial Power Loss • Brownouts or total outages can be related to natural disasters. • Voltage fluctuations can be weather related. • Loss of power can affect the organization's ability to process work due to the lack of electrically powered equipment, and the degradation of otherwise safe and comfortable facilities.	• Site files contain equipment specification data for all major electrical power system equipment. • Electrical equipment rooms are clean and organized. • On-site backup power is available. • The fuel supply for the emergency generator is sufficient for recovery of electrical power requirements. • The emergency generator fuel supply is changed regularly. • UPS and emergency generators are tested on a regular basis. • The facility has power-regulating equipment which smoothes power fluctuations. • Critical equipment is connected to a UPS system. • Power for the facility can be obtained from more than one utility substation. • Emergency lighting is available.
Floods • Can be caused by rivers, snow melt, heavy rains, dam failure, etc. • Can be accompanied by utility loss, structural damage, and civil disorder. • Paper and electronic media records are subject to damage. • Use of damaged equipment and records can lead to processing errors. • Loss of physical access. • Power disruption. • Cessation of business activities.	• The location and construction of the facility are such that they minimize the risk of damage from seepage from the floor or roof. • Paper documents are located in a waterproof environment. • The computer facility is located above the first floor. • Data and software are backed up and stored off-site at a location that is not susceptible to a flood that would damage the primary facility. • Plastic bags are available for paper records. • Flood levels are projected for strategy purposes.
HVAC Failure • Proper temperature and humidity are necessary for efficient operation of staff and equipment. • Ventilators and air conditioners can conduct flames and smoke in a fire.	• The facility uses redundant HVAC units. This spreads the cooling load among several systems. • Critical spare parts are kept on hand. • Adequate measures have been taken to combat static electricity.

Threats	Consequences	Preventive measures
	• Equipment can be damaged if temperature and humidity vary beyond an allowable range. • Ineffective filtering in air handlers can allow smoke and dust particles to damage equipment and magnetic media. • Bacteria can grow in air ducting and can contribute to serious health hazards for employees.	• Regular preventive maintenance is conducted with special attention to filters and the cleaning of ducting. • HVAC equipment is protected from other exposures such as fire, water, and sabotage.
Internal Plumbing Failure	• Can affect air conditioning, potable water supply, and bathroom water supply. • Can cause damage to paper, film, and magnetic media data records.	• Preventive maintenance is routinely conducted on the facility's water distribution system. • A system for rapid shutdown of the sprinkler system is in place in the event of an accidental activation of the system. • Tarps are available in areas exposed to sprinklers/pipes. • Dry charge sprinkler systems are used. • Water protection and alarm systems are in place under raised floors. • These systems are monitored around the clock. • The computer room has drains and/or pumps available to remove water. • Vital records are located in a waterproof environment.
Earthquake	• Can cause structural collapse or severe structural damage. • Can cause loss of public utilities. • Disruption of lives of staff, loss of life possible. • Widespread illness, civil disorder, etc. • Explosion and fire. • Broken water main—temporary flooding. • Loss of substation power.	• Earthquake construction guidelines have been adhered to so that damage can be minimized. • Equipment tie-downs are used on critical computer equipment. • Emergency power is available on site. • Seismic risk evaluations are done for all facilities in high-risk areas.

	• Loss of voice/data communications. • Damage to computer and switch. • Destruction of building.	
Water	• Loss of the water supply or its pollution can be caused by natural disaster. • Loss of the water supply increases the loss potential in the event of a fire. • Loss or pollution of the water supply can affect staff productivity. • Loss of the water supply for bathroom facilities will cause the total facility to be deemed unusable. • Contaminated wastewater discharge can bring fines and be injurious to the health of staff and non-staff.	• An emergency water supply has been contracted for in the event of an emergency. • Alarms to alert personnel of water shutdown have been installed. • Non-water fire suppression systems are available. • Effluent discharge control equipment capable of meeting the legal requirements for discharge has been installed. • A spill protection system has been installed to prevent and mitigate uncontrolled discharge to surface water, an effluent system, soil, air, or ground water.
Communications Carriers	• Movement to on-line, real-time systems has increased the exposure to communications problems. • Total or partial outages can be caused by natural disasters, weather, accident or sabotage. • Carriers are subject to penetration by unauthorized personnel.	• Alternate facilities that feed through a different telephone-switching center have been identified for use in the event of communications loss. • Alternate routing in the form of dial backup for leased lines has been installed. • Fiber optics rather than copper wire is used in order to avoid electromagnetic tapping and interference. • The facility is serviced by more than one telephone central office.
Transportation	• Partial or complete breakdowns can result from natural disasters, strikes, fuel shortages, inclement weather, etc. • Can disrupt movement of staff, supplies, mail, work, etc.	• There is a multitude of motels in the area to provide temporary housing in case staff members have to remain close to work. • Alternate means of moving mail have been identified. • Alternate facilities have been identified for use in the event this facility is inaccessible. • Alternate transportation vendors have been identified and contacted for use in an emergency situation.

Threats	Consequences	Preventive measures
Staff Productivity Risks	• Degraded environment, fatigue, sudden increase in volume, etc. can cause errors. • Shortage of staff due to illness, injury, job actions, transportation problems, chemical exposure, etc. can occur. • Key personnel may be absent. • A range of deliberate acts including theft, defalcation, deliberate disregard of procedures, and sabotage can occur. • Penalties, lawsuits, and loss of assets and data can result. • Falling can injure staff. • Machine stored energy can injure staff. • Staff can be injured by unrestrained equipment/materials. • Air quality can negatively impact staff health and productivity.	• The work areas and process designs are such that they maximize efficiency and comfort, and minimize fatigue and boredom. • Files are backed up and procedures are documented. • Anti-theft screws are used on PC covers. • An active asset management program is in place. • Bags are checked and authorization for computer equipment removal is required upon departing the facility. • There are procedures for equipment/software return upon termination of employment. • Proper training and necessary cross-training is given. • Potential employees and contractors are screened for substance abuse and for problems with previous employers. • Alternate sources of trained employees have been identified. • Qualified personnel have conducted qualitative and quantitative exposure assessments. • Equipment has been designed to control chemical/physical agent exposures below Occupational Exposure Guidelines. • Stairs, platforms and/or railings are provided where frequent access, carrying tools, or poking of railcars is required in a fall hazard area. • Lockable disconnect devices that directly interrupt electrical, pneumatic, hydraulic, gravity or any form of stored energy from equipment have been installed. • Equipment is guarded from moving equipment, extreme temperatures, and high velocity or high-pressure materials. • Restraint devices for trailers, trucks and rail cars are available. • Storage racks are designed to support the load, to protect the structure from collision, and to protect pallets from falling through the racks. • Air monitoring is performed, and respiratory protection is used where needed. • A behavior observation and feedback system has been implemented. • Enzyme levels are monitored and controlled through air sample analysis. • First Aid supplies are available. • Safety showers and eye wash fountains are available. • Noise levels are monitored and controlled.

People-Related Risks (External)	• Illegal intrusion resulting in theft, sabotage, tampering with equipment or data can occur. • Theft off-premises, such as robbery of messengers, can occur.	• Both human and electronic security are present in the building and in the Data Processing area. • Shredders are available for the destruction of sensitive materials. • Entry is monitored for "official business" visitors. • Photo ID badges are required. • Key cards or other methods of selective entry are required for admission to sensitive areas. • All external entry points to the building are monitored and have intrusion alarms. • Sensitive areas are locked at all times. • The operation has adequate insurance protection. • Physical security fences, gates, exterior lights, parking lots, etc. are maintained to prevent intrusion.
Plant Equipment Risk	• Improper installation could cause spills, explosions and other production-ending situations. • Gas cylinders could explode.	• Design and construction standards have been adhered to in equipment installation. • Environmental control equipment is capable of meeting regulatory requirements. • Performance data are assessed with regard to design intent. • Qualified assessors conduct combustion safety studies. • Materials of construction, fabrication quality, and maximum allowable pressure (MAP) of pressure vessels are verified as correct. • Gas cylinders have a storage facility and handling equipment.
Neighborhood Hazards	• The building is near an interstate highway where trucks routinely transport hazardous and toxic materials. • The building is near a large international airport.	• There is a nightly backup of data processing electronic record and that backup is stored off-site. • The off-site backup facility is a sufficient distance away from this facility. • An alternate site has been identified for use in the event that this facility is unusable.

Threats	Consequences	Preventive measures
Data Processing Risk	• Equipment loss, complete or partial, caused by power failure, HVAC failure, component breakdown, natural disaster, sabotage, etc. • Computer equipment failure. • Data loss or corruption. • Communications breakdown or errors. • Absence or loss of design, software and procedures documentation. • Unavailability of key personnel.	• Vendors have been identified who will deliver replacement equipment in the event of an emergency. • Preventive maintenance on all computer components is performed. • On-call field engineering support is available. • Provisions to switch (electrically) to backup/redundant equipment in the event of failure have been made (e.g. off-site mirrored hard drives). • The computer room is not adjacent to highly flammable materials. • External air/heat ducts, which enter rooms where business critical equipment/documents/magnetic media reside, are lined with non-combustible material. • Off-site backup of critical hardware, software, data files, documentation, forms and supplies, etc. are available. Backups are tested and/or reviewed regularly. • Warrantees and service agreements on vital equipment and software have been obtained. • Leased lines have a dial-up backup. • Contact with vendors has been made for rapid replacement of equipment after a disaster. • All magnetic media is tested for viruses. • There is adherence to the manufacturers' requirements and recommendations regarding the provision of power, environmental conditions, layout specifications, and other related information. • Special storage vaults on-site are used for critical tape and disk files. • Good housekeeping practices are used in the computer room. • Off-site storage provides adequate security, fire protection, and environmental considerations. • Access to files is controlled. • Records of removal and return of stored files are maintained. • Computer-dependent business units have established manual procedures.

| **People-Related Risks (Internal)** | • Dismissed staff can cause harm to records.
• Disgruntled employees can start fires, disrupt work-flows, and steal from the organization. | • Management permits employees to air grievances using open door policies.
• Employees are given regular performance appraisals and encouraged to discuss their feelings.
• Background checks are made on employees prior to hire.
• Immediately upon dismissal, an employee is removed from a sensitive area, access to secure areas is removed, and computer access passwords/sign-on for terminated staff is removed.
• There is control of access to programs, manual and/or automated files, and reports to those that must use or have access to them in performance of their work.
• Access to the operations area is controlled.
• Visitors are escorted when they are in operations areas. A control form from the operations area is used, which specifies reports sent and number of pages for each.
• Abnormal employee behavior is monitored. |

During the BIA process you will evaluate the risk of business process failures and will identify critical and necessary business functions and their resource dependencies. You will also:

- estimate the financial and operational impacts of a disruption,
- identify regulatory/compliance exposure, and
- determine the impact upon the client's market share and corporate image.

One result of the analysis is a determination of each business function's Recovery Time Objectives (RTO). The RTO is the amount of time allowed for the recovery of a business function. If the RTO is exceeded, then severe damage to the organization would result. These time estimates and dollar contributions of the business unit allow management to make an informed decision on how to allocate recovery funds. Additionally, the BIA process allows Information Services to have an RTO determined for applications that support the critical business units.

Based upon the results of the BIA, you can perform a review of additional expense and business interruption insurance coverage required by the organization.

What does the BIA process provide to the organization? It

- provides an independent view of risks from a disaster situation,
- provides a basis for determining cost-effective strategies,
- determines critical and necessary business functions/processes and their resource dependencies,
- identifies critical computer applications and the associated outage tolerance,
- estimates the financial and operational impact of the disruption and the required recovery time frame for the critical business functions, and finally
- builds a business case for strategy selection.

The first step in conducting a BIA is to identify all business units within the organization, using a confirmed Organization Chart. Whether or not you think the business unit is important, an interview must be conducted.

The next step is to design a customized questionnaire. An example of a questionnaire follows:

BUSINESS IMPACT ANALYSIS

BUSINESS:_____

DATE: _____

CONTACT: _____

DEPARTMENT: _____

PRODUCT / SERVICE NAME: _____

DESCRIPTION OF DEPARTMENT FUNCTIONS:

_____

_____

_____

_____

_____

_____

_____

_____

_____

DEPENDENCIES:

Vendors: (Name)   (Service/Product)

_____   _____

_____   _____

_____   _____

_____   _____

_____   _____

_____   _____

Software: (Name)   (Vendor)

_____   _____

_____   _____

_____   _____

_____   _____

_____   _____

Department:(Name)   (Service/Product)

_____   _____

_____   _____

_____   _____

_____   _____

_____   _____

Who are your primary customers?
(Name)   (Name)

_____   _____
_____   _____
_____   _____
_____   _____
_____   _____
_____   _____

Upon which computer platforms do you depend (PC, Server, Mid-range, Main-Frame)?

How long can this department continue operations via manual means? _____

Explain: _____

_____
_____

> In the following section, use the listed criteria to indicate at what point in time the loss of this service would begin to have a significant impact upon the financial well-being of the organization.

POTENTIAL EFFECTS OF DISRUPTION: **DURATION OF OUTAGE**

Affect	<1day	1–2 days	2–5 days	5–10 days	>10 days
Direct loss of **Net Income**					
Quantify ($):					
Decrease in **Customer Service**					
Increased **Operating Expense** (Overtime, Vendor Expense)					
Exposure to **Contractual Fines/Penalties**					
Loss of **Staff Productivity**					
Exposure to **Litigation and Adverse Awards**					
Inability to **Service Other Business Units**					

What are the most critical times of the Week, Month, Year? _____
_____

Has there ever been a disaster here?   Explain: _____
_____

What types of insurance does this organization have (type and $ limits)?

Resource Items

The Resource Item Questionnaire should be used in conjunction with a walk-around of the business unit. Remember to refer back to the business unit flow chart and other sections of the BIA. By in-depth probing in the Resource Item section, many bits of information relevant to the recovery can be unearthed.

(Normal refers to quantities currently on hand, Minimal refers to the minimum quantity required to perform the business unit's critical functions.)

Items	Normal	Minimum
Data Communications		
128 K Data Lines		
256K Data Lines		
56K Data Lines		
T-1 Lines		
Facilities		
Meeting Rooms (10 × 20)		
Office Space (100 sq. ft./person)		
Storage Space		
Vehicles		
Microcomputers		
Check Printers		
Personal Computers		
Printers		
Scanners		
Surge Protectors		
UPS		
Office Equipment		
Calculator		
Copier		
Fax		
Postage Meter/Scales		

Shredder		
Typewriter		
Office Furniture		
Chairs		
Computer Racks		
Desks		
File Cabinets		
Tables		
Off-Site Storage		
Account system backup		
Blank Checks		
LAN backup		
Payroll backup		
SOFTWARE		
Microsoft Office		
Lotus Notes		
Staff		
Accountants		
Clerical		
Controller		
Customer Service Representative		
Data Entry Clerk		
IS Director		
Marketing Executive		
Network Systems Analyst		
Payroll Clerk		
Receptionist		
Secretary		

Systems Engineer		
Typist		
Word Processor		
Supplies		
Copy Paper		
Folders		
Diskettes		
Telecommunications		
Mobile Phones		
Pagers		
PBX/Centrex		
Telephone Console		
Telephones		

Armed with the BIA interview form, you should interview all key business personnel. The interview process should take about 45 minutes to an hour to complete. After the interview it is important to write up the results of the interview and send it back to the interviewee to ensure that all that was said was heard. The write-up should look something like the following:

FINANCIAL SERVICES

Location: Southfield, Illinois

First Draft Date: 06/18/01   Last Revision Date: 06/18/01

Key Business Function:
- Financial Reporting and Control

Vendors:
- Great Plains
- PricewaterhouseCoopers
- Deloitte Touche
- Marsh & McLennan
- AON

Applications:
- Great Plains
- Windows Office

Internal Dependencies:
- All Departments

Primary Customers:
- (See List)
- Employees

Platforms:
- Personal Computers
- LAN
- VAX

Critical Timing:
- Month-end
- Year-end

Recovery Window:
- More than 10 days

Respondent: James Borinsky   **Telephone: 555-555-5555**

Overview of Area:
The Financial Services department is comprised of the Controller function, Human Resources, Facilities, and Facilities Security. Since most of these functions are discussed in other BIA documents, only the Controller function will be discussed here.

The Controller function is responsible for internal and external financial reporting, Accounts Payable, Accounts Receivable, Budget, Forecasting, Fixed Assets, and Investments.

Financial Impact:
Loss of this function would not have a significant immediate impact upon the financial well-being of the COMPANY X. In the event of a loss of the function, there would be a loss of the ability financially to manage the institution.

An additional touch that adds to the understanding of the process flow of the business unit is the addition of a process flow chart using a tool such a Visio.

Once all the individual reports are completed and confirmed by the business units, a preliminary report (which includes the Risk Assessment and the BIAs) should be prepared and sent to the organization's management for review. The report should contain:

- An inventory of critical business processes
- An evaluation of existing risk reduction measures
- Recommendations to enhance risk reduction measures

- An estimate of the potential financial and operational impact of a disruption on the critical business processes
- Identification of Recovery Time Objectives (RTO) for each critical business process
- A determination of minimum resources required by critical business functions during recovery operations.

Once all the problems with the document are resolved, a final report and presentation should be prepared and presented to the organization's management. The following is a template format for that report:

MANAGEMENT SUMMARY AND BACKGROUND

The COMPANY (TC) is committed to the development of a BCP that will develop strategies for the recovery of the organization's functionality. While TC has procedures in place to keep its computerized systems continuously running, it requires a plan to recover from a wider range of disasters. Accordingly, a planning engagement was started on the 30 June, 2001 for the COMPANY. The plan will be designed to document the recovery of the COMPANY's functionality at the 40 South Street, South Bend, Indiana facility.

In our initial examination, we found the following major threats/risks that could delay a recovery:

- The COMPANY does not have an emergency generator to provide electrical power in the event that commercial power becomes unavailable. This risk is somewhat mitigated by the Company's access to two independent power grids and an extensive battery power reserve. However, in the event of an area-wide disaster, access to electrical power and the ability to maintain the operating capacity of the COMPANY would be at risk.
- An alternate, production-ready site is currently not available in the event that the 40 South Street, South Bend, Indiana facility becomes incapacitated. Without a pre-arranged site, the acquisition of an alternate site complete with adequate space, computer equipment, and communications connectivity would require several months of focused effort.

We have completed our initial Risk Assessment and Business Impact Analysis. We offer the following high level recommendations:

- Utilize the existing Disaster Recovery Plan as a reference for Business Continuity Planning. Continue the Business Continuity Process by enhancing the BCP as new technologies are incorporated by the COMPANY.
- Act on risk mitigation recommendations from this document.
- Institute a recovery alternative/facility that will enable business resumption of the COMPANY's critical functions as emerging technologies permit.
- Commit to annual BCP exercises upon initial completion of plan(s) documentation.
- Foster and actively promote business-wide awareness of Business Continuity/Disaster Recovery and encourage active participation by employees at all levels.

- Protect documents and magnetic media from water damage.
- Remove housekeeping-related hazards from computer rooms and other work areas.
- Document procedures for the recovery of computerized operating systems.
- Maintain the proactive attention to risk mitigation.

For a more detailed explanation of our recommendations, please see the recommendations section of this document.

We have identified processes that are critical. During our interviews with each of the COMPANY's departments, we asked the question: "After what period of time (duration), would the loss of your function have a critical impact upon the financial well-being of the COMPANY?" The outage durations considered were 0–2 days, 2–5 days, 5–10 days, and more than 10 days. The following "Recovery Window Analysis" identifies the relative criticality of functions and their implied recovery windows:

Recovery Window Analysis

Division	Duration of Outage until Critical Impact			
	0–2 Days	**2–5 Days**	**5–10 Days**	**>10 Days**
Marketing/Ops				
		Customer Service & Systems Support		
				National Sales
	Marketing/Public Relations			
	Trading Floor Ops.			
Market Regulation/ Legal				
	Market Structure			
				Legal & Office of the Secretary
			Market Regulation	
			Market Regulation/ Surveillance	
		Listing		
Financial Services				
				Accounting Services
				Human Resources
				Facility's Security
Information Systems				
		Applications Development		
	IS Support Services			
	IS Operations			
	Data/Telecomm/IS Facilities			

Risk Assessment Objectives

- Quantify, to the extent possible, the potential business impacts to the COMPANY from a disruption to normal business activities.
- Reassess current disaster recovery strategies and established recovery timeframes.
- Simplify decision-making process during a stressful situation.
- Suggest procedural change where necessary.
- Identify legal and regulatory issues related to a business interruption.
- Identify and address critical business functions, operations, facilities, departments and their respective resource support systems and requirements.

Continuing Project Objectives

- Outline the steps required to minimize the length of an interruption to critical business functions. This implies strategies that will be explored in the next phase of this engagement. At this point, potential strategies identified for examination include:
  —Acquisition of a functional alternate facility.
  —Acquisition of an emergency electricity generator.
  —Recover TC functionality as efficiently as possible without the aid of a functional alternate facility or electricity generator.
- Describe the resources required for the recovery of the COMPANY's systems and business units subsequent to a disruption.
- Identify the COMPANY's requirements to continue its mission to provide quality service on a timely basis.
- Identify other viable resource recovery alternatives.
- Develop and implement an efficient and effective BCP for each business component.
- Develop an efficient plan maintenance scheme and effectively automate the documentation process.
- Communicate and keep all employees current on plan information and individual responsibilities.
- Protect the COMPANY employees.

Project Scope and Assumptions

The following assumptions pertain to the BCP, as a whole:

- This project addresses the risk involved with a disruption to business operations of the COMPANY South Bend facility.
- The analysis is based on business operations as of June 1999.
- The BCP will be written to address worst case scenarios.
- This phase of the project includes assessing business risks and determining the COMPANY's vulnerability to a loss of computing resources or business units that the organization depends on for daily operation.

The following assumptions pertain specifically to the development of the BCP:

- The affected location will be rendered inoperative and inaccessible.
- Some personnel will survive the disaster and will be available for recovery implementation.
- Only the 110 North Front Street facility is considered.
- Recovery of the services provided by the COMPANY is the sole focus of the BCP.
- Once developed, guidelines for off-site storage of data, supplies and documentation have been strictly followed. Items stored off-site are intact and accessible.
- Recovery team leaders have accepted and acted upon their responsibilities.
- The BCP will serve as a set of guidelines, not absolute rules. It is not all-inclusive. Decisions not expressly documented within are to be made by the Management team during the recovery process.

Project Activities

The Business Impact Analysis project included interviewing key individuals to gain a better understanding of what functions are performed in each department and what the financial impact on the COMPANY would be if a disaster occurred. We sought to understand the impacts on the COMPANY if these departments ceased to function. To accomplish this, we examined the effects upon: net income, customer service, operating expenses, adverse awards and penalties, productivity, and collateral departmental effects.

To carry out this analysis, we conducted interviews with representatives of all major departments of the COMPANY (see BIA RESULTS). It was through this process that the business impact of a disaster was assessed.

We have positioned COMPANY personnel to work with us on future steps of the project, such as the identification of recovery resource requirements, the development of disaster recovery teams and a review of potential recovery sites. Additionally, we made immediate mitigation recommendations intended to reduce exposures and enhance disaster preparedness. The recommendations are listed in the "Strengths and Concerns" section of this document.

We conducted a walk-through inspection of the COMPANY to understand business operations better and to identify potential areas of risk resulting from physical control weaknesses.

We have provided the COMPANY with a Physical Security Assessment document that was completed by the COMPANY personnel under our guidance. Recommendations were noted.

We have analyzed the accumulated information and have formulated suggested recovery timeframes.

We have also performed a vulnerability and threat analysis for the facilities and have identified the departmental recovery priorities.

Initial Findings

From our initial project activities, we have identified the following findings regarding disaster history, disaster threats and specific vulnerabilities.

Disaster History
The COMPANY has not, in recent memory, been forced to close. The South Bend flood of 1992 did not have an effect on the operations of the Company.

Risk Assessment
The chart on the following pages provides information concerning documented threats and their likelihood. This chart also provides the vulnerability and consequences of each threat.

Strengths and Concerns

Strengths
- Electrical power redundancies
- Communications redundancies
- Internal computerized system redundancies
- Effective crisis management team structure
- Tremendous attention to fire suppression
- Outstanding facility security

Concerns
- Documents and magnetic media are unprotected from water damage. We recommend that plastic bags/tarps be made available to protect these documents and magnetic media.
- Boxes and other potentially flammable materials are stored in the computer room. We recommend that housekeeping-related hazards be removed from computer rooms.
- Some IS Division offices have boxes blocking aisles so that in the event of a fire, staff would be hindered in their attempt to evacuate the building. We recommend that passageways in office work areas be cleared to allow for rapid staff egress in the event of an emergency.
- Computer system operating/recovery procedures, vendor/staff contact information, and vital schematics and drawings are maintained in various locations throughout the organization. We recommend that a comprehensive Systems Administrator's Manual containing this critical information be assembled and a copy maintained off-site.
- In the event of a disaster or during periodic emergency situations, documentation of network operating systems is not sufficient to efficiently restore network capabilities. We recommend a better documentation of network operating systems and redundancies be developed. A copy of the documentation should be stored off-site.
- On-site backup tapes are stored in open racks within the computer room. In the event of an isolated event in the computer room, both the on-line systems and the most current tape backups would be at risk. We recommend that the on-site tape storage be separated from the computer room and have available fire and water protection/suppression similar to that of the computer room.

Threats	Consequences	Preventive measures	Likelihood
Severe Storms	• Can be accompanied by flooding, loss of utilities, structural damage, falling trees, etc. • Use of damaged equipment and records can lead to processing errors. • Can delay or prevent staff from reaching work. • Loss of physical access. • Cessation of business activities.	• The building is constructed to meet local and state building codes. • Plastic bags are available to protect documents and magnetic media. • Vital records and all data processing facilities are located above the first floor which protects them from flooding. • Cross-training is an on-going process. This guards against the loss of staff. • There is a multitude of motels in the area to provide temporary housing in case staff members have to remain close to work.	HIGH
Fire/Explosion	• Can be the direct or indirect result of other natural disasters. • Can be caused by equipment failure, accident or sabotage. • Water and other damage can occur while fighting the fire. • Facilities can be destroyed or rendered unusable for an extended period. • Processing can be interrupted for an extended period. • Assets and vital records can be lost. • The business can be interrupted with resulting penalty interest and legal claims. • Loss of voice/data communications • Personnel injuries and/or deaths	• Fire/smoke detection systems are in place and are monitored on a continual basis. • Air ducts are equipped with power dampers to prevent/minimize smoke migration. • The computer room is configured to minimize the extent of fire damage (kill switches are on sprinklers so that power in the computer room goes off before water spays). • Fire suppression systems in the form of fire extinguishers and sprinkler systems are found throughout the building on every floor. • Fire extinguishers are found near the exits of the computer room. • Employees are trained in fire-fighting equipment. • Employees are trained in emergency shut down procedures. • Employees are trained in reporting emergencies. • Employees are trained in evacuation procedures. • Exit routes are posted and exit route signs are found throughout the building. • Preventive maintenance is performed on potentially hazardous equipment. • Blank paper stock is not permitted in the computer room except for the current day's requirement.	HIGH

- Cleaning compounds are not permitted in the computer room except for the current day's requirement.
- Oils and fuels are not permitted in the computer room except for the current day's requirement.
- Printed materials and garbage are removed from the computer room on a regular basis.
- Combustible materials are stored in areas suited for that function.
- There are procedures for fire department notification.
- The fire department has toured and has a diagram of the facility.
- The area under the raised floor is cleaned regularly.
- The building is constructed to reduce the potential for fire.
- The building is located away from potential hazards which could restrict access of the fire department.
- There are no housekeeping related hazards.
- There are crash bars on emergency exit doors.
- Emergency exits/routes/lighting/alarms are checked and tested regularly.
- Locks in the computer room release when the fire alarm sounds.
- Closets and unused areas are equipped with fire/smoke detection and alarm systems.
- Tile lifters are available in raised floor environments to investigate alarm conditions and fire suppression.
- Macros are available for the rapid shutdown of systems.
- Backup tapes and the System Administrator's Manual can be assembled and carried off site in a very rapid manner.
- Backup copies of vital magnetic media are securely stored off-site.
- Backup copies of vital paper records are securely stored off-site or maintained in a fireproof environment.

Threats	Consequences	Preventive measures	Likelihood
Communi-cations Carriers	• Movement to on-line, real-time systems has increased the exposure to communications problems. • Total or partial outages can be caused by natural disasters, weather, accident or sabotage. • Carriers are subject to penetration by unauthorized personnel.	• Alternate facilities that feed through a different telephone-switching center have been identified for use in the event of communications loss. • Alternate routing in the form of dial backup for leased lines has been installed. • Fiber optics rather than copper wire is used in order to avoid electromagnetic tapping and interference. • The facility is serviced by more than one telephone-switching center.	HIGH
People-Related Risks (Internal)	• Degraded environment, fatigue, sudden increase in volume, etc. can cause errors. • Shortage of staff due to illness, injury, job actions, transportation problems. etc. can occur. • Key personnel may be absent. • A range of deliberate acts including theft, defalcation, deliberate disregard of procedures, and sabotage can occur. • Penalties, lawsuits, and loss of assets and data can result. • Dismissed staff can cause harm to records. • Disgruntled employees can start fires, disrupt work flows, and steal from the organization.	• The work areas and process designs are such that they maximize efficiency and comfort, and minimize fatigue and boredom. • Files are backed up and procedures are documented. • Anti-theft screws are used on PC covers. • An active asset management program is in place. • Bags are checked and authorization for computer equipment removal is required upon departing the facility. • There are procedures for equipment/software return upon termination of employment. • Proper training and necessary cross-training is given. • Potential employees and contractors are screened for substance abuse and for problems with previous employers. • Alternate sources of trained employees have been identified. • Management permits employees to air grievances using open door policies. • Employees are given regular performance appraisals and encouraged to discuss their feelings. • Background checks are made on employees prior to hire. • Immediately upon dismissal, an employee is removed from a sensitive area, access to secure areas is removed, and computer access passwords/sign-on for terminated staff is removed.	HIGH

Risk Category	Risks	Controls	Rating
		• There is control of access to programs, manual and/or automated files, and reports to those that must use or have access to them in performance of their work. • Access to the operations area is controlled. • Visitors are escorted when they are in operations areas.	
People-Related Risks (External)	• Illegal intrusion resulting in theft, sabotage, tampering with equipment or data can occur. • Theft off-premises, such as robbery of messengers, can occur.	• Both human and electronic security are present in the building and in the Data Processing area. • Shredders are available for the destruction of sensitive materials. • Entry is monitored for "official business" visitors. • Photo ID badges are required. • Key cards or other methods of selective entry are required for admission to sensitive areas. • All external entry points to the building are monitored and have intrusion alarms. • Sensitive areas are locked at all times. • The operation has adequate insurance protection.	HIGH
Data Processing Risk	• Equipment loss, complete or partial, caused by power failure, HVAC failure, component breakdown, natural disaster, sabotage, etc. • Computer equipment failure. • Data loss or corruption. • Communications breakdown or errors. • Absence or loss of design, software and procedures documentation. • Unavailability of key personnel.	• Vendors have been identified who will deliver replacement equipment in the event of an emergency. • Preventive maintenance on all computer components is performed. • On-call field engineering support is available. • Provisions to switch (electrically) to backup/redundant equipment in the event of failure have been made (e.g. off-site mirrored hard drives). • The computer room is not adjacent to highly flammable materials. • External air/heat ducts, which enter rooms where business critical equipment/documents/magnetic media reside, are lined with non-combustible material. • Off-site backup of critical hardware, software, data files, documentation, forms and supplies, etc. are available. Backups are tested and/or reviewed regularly.	HIGH

Threats	Consequences	Preventive measures	Likelihood
		• Warrantees and service agreements on vital equipment and software have been obtained. • Leased lines have a dial-up backup. • Contact with vendors has been made for rapid replacement of equipment after a disaster. • All magnetic media is tested for viruses. • There is adherence to the manufacturers' requirements and recommendations regarding the provision of power, environmental conditions, layout specifications, and other related information. • Special storage vaults on-site are used for critical tape and disk files. • Good housekeeping practices are used in the computer room. • Off-site storage provides adequate security, fire protection, and environmental considerations. • Access to files is controlled. • Records of removal and return of stored files are maintained.	
Commercial Power Loss	• Brownouts or total outages can be related to natural disasters. • Voltage fluctuations can be weather related. • Loss of power can affect the organization's ability to process work due to the lack of electrically powered equipment, and the degradation of otherwise safe and comfortable facilities.	• On-site backup power is available. • The fuel supply for the emergency generator is sufficient for recovery of electrical power requirements. • UPS and emergency generators are tested on a regular basis. • The facility has power-regulating equipment which smoothes power fluctuations. • Critical equipment is connected to an uninterrupted power source (UPS) system. • Power for the facility can be obtained from more than one utility substation.	MODERATE

Internal Plumbing Failure	• Can affect air conditioning, potable water supply, and bathroom water supply. • Can cause damage to paper, film, and magnetic media data records.	• Preventive maintenance is routinely conducted on the facility's water distribution system. • A system for rapid shutdown of the sprinkler system is in place in the event of an accidental activation of the system. • Tarps are available in areas exposed to sprinklers/pipes. • Dry charge sprinkler systems are used. • Water protection and alarm systems are in place under raised floors. These systems are monitored around the clock. • The computer room has drains and/or pumps available to remove water. • Vital records are located in a waterproof environment.	MODERATE
Transportation	• Partial or complete breakdowns can result from natural disasters, strikes, fuel shortages, inclement weather, etc. • Can disrupt movement of staff, supplies, mail, work, etc.	• There is a multitude of motels in the area to provide temporary housing in case staff members have to remain close to work. • Alternate means of moving mail have been identified. • Alternate facilities have been identified for use in the event this facility is inaccessible.	MODERATE
Neighborhood Hazards	• The building is near an interstate highway where trucks routinely transport hazardous and toxic materials. • The building is near a large international airport. • A major road passes under the trading floor of the company.	• There is a nightly backup of data processing electronic record and that backup is stored off-site. • The off-site backup facility is a sufficient distance away from this facility. • An alternate site has been identified for use in the event that this facility is unusable.	MODERATE

Threats	Consequences	Preventive measures	Likelihood
Internal Electrical Power	• Transients caused by variations in building load can occur. • Failure of power distribution system can occur. • Can cause processing failures. • Can cause equipment damage and excessive downtime.	• Emergency lights have been installed. • In the event of a loss of commercial electricity, electric power can be maintained through emergency generators located at the facility. • The power from the emergency generator can maintain the organization's vital functions. • Circuits are protected by circuit breakers. • Cords/wiring are kept in good shape. • UPS equipment is used throughout the building. • UPS system is monitored around the clock. • Exit lights are clearly visible. • Procedures are in place to recover from a power failure. • Preventive maintenance of emergency power equipment is routinely conducted. • Power distribution systems are protected from hazards such as fire, water, accident, and sabotage.	LOW
Floods	• Can be caused by rivers, snow melt, heavy rains, dam failure, etc. • Can be accompanied by utility loss, structural damage, and civil disorder. • Paper and electronic media records are subject to damage. • Use of damaged equipment and records can lead to processing errors. • Loss of physical access. • Power disruption. • Cessation of business activities.	• The location and construction of the facility are such that they minimize the risk of damage from seepage from the floor or roof.	LOW

Threat	Description	Controls	Rating
HVAC Failure	• Proper temperature and humidity are necessary for efficient operation of staff and equipment. • Ventilators and air conditioners can conduct flames and smoke in a fire. • Equipment can be damaged if temperature and humidity vary beyond an allowable range. • Ineffective filtering in air handlers can allow smoke and dust particles to damage equipment and magnetic media. • Bacteria can grow in air ducting and can contribute to serious health hazards for employees.	• The facility uses redundant HVAC units. This spreads the cooling load among several systems. • Critical spare parts are kept on hand. • Adequate measures have been taken to combat static electricity. • Regular preventive maintenance is conducted with special attention to filters and the cleaning of ducting. • HVAC equipment is protected from other exposures such as fire, water, and sabotage.	LOW
Earthquake	• Can cause structural collapse or severe structural damage. • Can cause loss of public utilities. • Disruption of lives of staff; loss of life possible. • Widespread illness, civil disorder, etc. • Explosion and fire. • Broken water main—temporary flooding. • Loss of substation power. • Loss of voice/data communications. • Damage to computer and switch. • Destruction of building.	• Earthquake construction guidelines have been adhered to so that damage can be minimized. • Equipment tie-downs are used on critical computer equipment. • Emergency power is available on-site.	LOW

Insurance Coverage

The COMPANY Insurance Program is as follows:

Insurance Type	Policy Number	Effective Date	Expiry Date		Limits
Real and Business Pers. Property business Income and Accounts Receivable: *Not to exceed the following sub-limits:*	ASV015076	10/15/98	10/15/99	General Aggregate	$126,677,950
Business Income including Extra Expense				Includes Extra Expenses	$76,000,000
Property in Transit					$25,000
Expediting Cost					$25,000
Consequential Loss					$2,500,000
Accounts Receivable					$15,000
Valuable Papers					$25,000
Inventory or Appraisal					$100,000
Personal Property of Officers or Employees					$25,000
Errors or Omissions					$100,000
Loss to Objects					$25,000,000
Ammonia Contamination					$25,000
Fine Arts					$55,000
Sewers or Drains					$5,000,000
Flood					$5,000,000
Earthquake					$5,000,000
General Liability: • General Aggregate Limit • Products/Completed Operations • Personal & Advertising Injury • Medical Expenses • Employee Benefits Errors & Omissions					$2,000,000 $2,000,000 $1,000,000 $ 10,000 $1,000,000

Listed Deductibles:

Earthquake	$50,000
Flood	$50,000
Sewer Backup	$50,000
Loss to Objects	$2,500
Consequential Loss	$5,000
All Other Cause of Loss	$1,000

Company: Royal & Sun Alliance
Broker: Aon Risk Services, Inc of Illinois
      1717 N. Naper Blvd. 3rd Floor
      Naperville, Ill 60563
      630–955–0357
      Debbie Campbell, CIC
(SOURCE: Brian Malone .... COMPANY)

No significant issues for Insurance were identified.

Recovery Window Analysis

The COMPANY authorized this Business Continuity Study to identify and develop business continuity strategies for recovery of the COMPANY's functionality. Based upon interviews conducted, the sequence in which departments should be recovered in the event of a disaster is listed in the following pages. Recovery priorities are based on respondents' information and both tangible and intangible considerations obtained from the surveys and interview process.

Continuity strategies and plans will be created based upon this analysis.

The following are the recovery windows for each department to recover its critical business functions and applications. Recovery sequences are defined as follows:

Zero to two days
Two to five days
Five to ten days
More than ten days

A list of functional areas (departments), their recovery priorities and recovery windows can be found on the following pages. The analysis of recovery timeframes was done with the understanding that the recovery environment is not "business as usual." Non-critical business functions will be recovered as appropriate after all the critical functions that are defined in this analysis are recovered.

(The rest of the report should contained the finalized and approved department interview forms.)

CONCLUSIONS

There are several key factors that are required to make the Business Assessment phase of the engagement successful. First, there must be senior management commitment to the process. Without that, you will find it very hard to get interviews and the required information in an efficient manner.

Second, you must use an effective survey questionnaire. If questions are asked that are irrelevant to the process or take too much time, then the client will lose faith and patience with the process. This can lead to an abrupt end to the engagement.

Third, emphasize that this process is *not* rightsizing! Emphasize that the information being gathered is only for the sake of a recovery effort in the event of a disaster, nothing else.

Fourth, all department functions must be represented in the interview process, not just Information Systems. In a recovery effort, reviving the computer systems is an important component, but without the other business units the organization would probably not be able to provide its product or service to its customers.

Fifth, interviews must be with the appropriate staff. It is advisable to interview the business unit's executive. This person will have the best knowledge of what is required to operate the unit. The executive may have other staff members as part of the interview, but he or she must be present.

Sixth, accept what the client says and do not argue. If the client insists that a coffee service is a critical resource for getting work done, then include coffee service as a resource item. If the client contends that their business unit has an RTO of 2 hours, then enter 2 hours and let the CEO or senior reviewing executive be the final judge.

Finally, the results must be reviewed with the CEO or highest executive available. Based on the senior executive's comments, the findings should be modified.

4

Strategy Selection

The objective of Strategy Selection is to assist the client in defining the action items needed to protect the organization and to select the most appropriate recovery solutions for critical business functions and supporting resources. The Strategy Selection process addresses a single point of failure (e.g. one production location, vendor dependency, one call center). It also addresses environmental risks (e.g. political instability, weather, earthquakes, etc.).

In the previous chapter, we identified the Recovery Time Objective (RTO) of each function of the business. In a three function company, the recovery time requirements might look like Figure 4.1. Each function of the company might have a different RTO. Therefore, the strategy to recover each function is encased in a different time requirement.

In the selection of a strategy, you must weigh the cost of being without the service at various points in time (the duration of the outage) against the cost of the solution. The objective is to minimize the total cost of the impact and the solution. I have attempeted to visualize this concept in Figure 4.2.

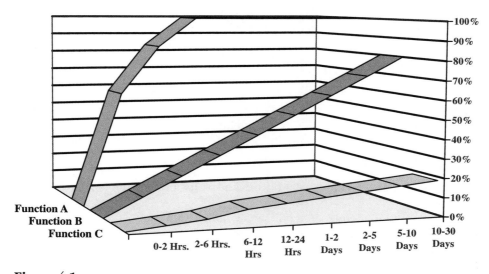

Figure 4.1

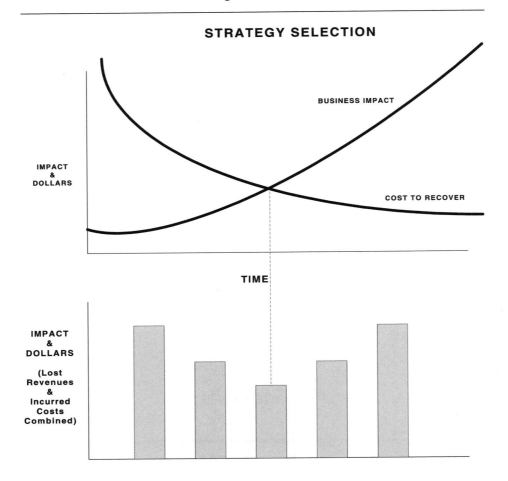

Figure 4.2   Strategy selection

Strategy alternatives are developed to define/refine the minimum resource re-quirements for recovery (i.e. alternate site profile). They include consideration of the following:

- Computer room capability—hardware and software operations, information networking
- Business unit independence (consistency of hardware/software)
- Communications requirements (voice and data)
- Work area requirements (space, equipment, supplies, vital records, etc.)
- Staffing levels
- Geography and transportation

COMPUTER CENTER RECOVERY

One of the most common strategies is the selection of a method of recovering computer capabilities. The strategy selections include: internal recovery, commercial hot-site/cold-site arrangements, reciprocal agreements, interim and/or manual procedures, reduction of service response, or suspension of services. Alternatives are heavily dependent upon the identified recovery time objectives. The less time available for the recovery, the more toward the top of the above list you must move. This also implies a greater cost. This cost must be weighed against the "bet on the table" or the profitability impact of the loss of service. Figure 4.3 shows the IT strategies that are available and the RTO that they satisfy.

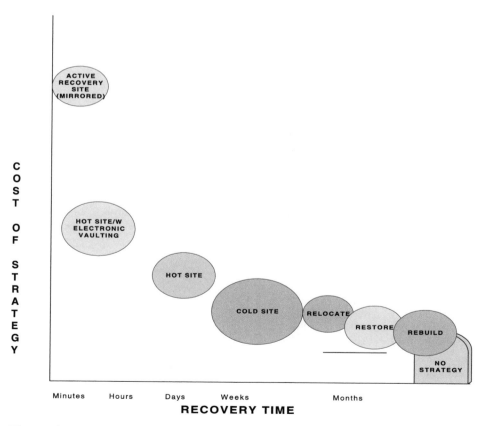

Figure 4.3

No Strategy

The least expensive strategy is to have no recovery or backup strategy. With this choice, data are not sent off-site, and there is no alternate site identified. There is no planned recovery document and any type of recovery will be accomplished by using on-site backups. Many times, organizations in this category use some type of incremental backup or physical volume backup method.

Relocate, Rebuild, Restore

The relocate, restore, rebuild strategies are, by themselves, insufficient to meet the needs of today's businesses. However, plans to return the organization to a pre-disaster state must include components. In an area-wide disaster such as a hurricane, it is important to have vendors that will facilitate these three functions so that they can be called immediately following the disaster. In wide area disasters, vendor resources become scarce. The first few to contact the vendor will get service, all others will wait, perhaps for weeks.

Cold Site

A cold site is generally a facility that contains a raised floor space, redundant power, and HVAC (heating, ventilation, air conditioning, cooling). If a disaster occurs, the organization obtains the necessary data processing equipment and installs it at the cold site.

This strategy has relatively low cost, but it is cumbersome to manage and the recovery time (RTO) is quite long. Because of today's dwindling RTOs, this strategy is becoming less acceptable.

Hot-Site

Commercial hot-sites are designed to recover a computer facility within 24 to 48 hours after an event. To accomplish this current backup tapes/disks must be available and a duplicate computer system/operating system/program set/ communication network (hot-site) must be immediately available. The leading vendors for this service are IBM, Sungard, and Comdisco. While less expensive than a fully redundant computer operation, this option can easily cost tens of thousands of dollars a month. To get an accurate estimate of the cost and the services provided by various vendors, you should assist the client in developing a Request for Proposal (RFP) to be submitted to each of the vendor candidates. The following is a sample RFP:

ABCD Company

REQUEST FOR PROPOSAL

I. INTRODUCTION

A. Organizational Overview

The ABCD Company has been established to provide a quality line of products to its customers. Among ABCD's products are X Y and Z.

The Headquarters for ABCD is located in CITY, STATE. This facility acts as the focal point for the organization and also houses the ABCD data center.

B. Purpose

ABCD is currently engaged in the development of a BCP. As part of this process, ABCD has reviewed its business applications to determine those which are absolutely essential to the running of its business and would need to be supported at an alternate site in the event of a disaster. ABCD has made a determination of the minimum facility and system resources required to run those critical applications.

In the event of a disaster, ABCD intends to have the communications abilities restored within 2 days after the declaration of a disaster. Along with the restoration of the communications abilities, ABCD also intends to re-locate up to 150 employees at an alternate work area site. This site will need to provide telephones, computer connections and working space for these 150 individuals.

Within 2 days after declaring a disaster, ABCD intends to restore their Local Area Network to provide access to all critical applications that will be used by ABCD. ABCD is planning to have PC terminals for all employees who will be located at the alternate work area site.

As a result, ABCD has issued this RFP for business continuity services. The intent of this document is to define the parameters and requirements of the desired business continuity services. Vendors are requested to review their capability to meet this timeframe through the supply of a hot-site and work area capability.

A hot-site is deemed to be a fully equipped and operational data processing facility capable of meeting ABCD's minimum resource requirements. It must contain not only the required computer equipment, but also all of the necessary support facilities including power, chillers, air conditioners, telecommunications equipment and lines, etc.

The work area site must have the ability to appropriately provide space for up to 150 employees to continue the operations of the organization. The office space should provide for desk space, computer connections, PCs and telephones for all the employees. In addition, it must have the needed support equipment including fax machine and copiers.

In the event of an extended outage, ABCD intends to install equipment into a contracted cold site. A cold site is deemed to be an empty computer room ready to receive and support a replacement computer configuration equivalent to that set out in this RFP. It is preferable that the cold site be co-located with the hot-site facility.

C. Recovery Configuration Specifications

Based upon the project which ABCD has performed to identify its needs in the event of a disaster, the vendor will be required to provide and maintain a fully

equipped hot-site and work area facility, including as a minimum the system configuration set out below. Vendors should indicate in their response their compliance or
non-compliance with each item. Variances should be identified and documented.
Alternate solutions may also be presented for consideration including telecommunications equipment and configurations (e.g. high-end Cisco routers, termination
of client owned T1 lines at the recovery site).

1. Computer Hardware
a. IBM RS/6000
Processors:

	CPU Model	Memory	Disk	Adapters
HRMS/FLS97 Peoplesoft DB Srvr	SP2 Wide Node 1 CPU	512 Mb	2 – 2.2Gb SCSI 1 – 4.5Gb SCSI 18 – 2.2Gb SSA	keyboard diskette 8-port async 3 high perf Ethernet std I/O parallel port tablet mouse HPS communications 2 SSA enhanced wide SCSI I/O
USPAN/fls96/Tfls/Dfls Peoplesoft DB Srvr	SP2 Wide Node 1 CPU	512 Mb	2 – 2.2Gb SCSI 1 – 4.5Gb SCSI 12 – 2.2Gb SSA	keyboard diskette 8-port async 3 high perf Ethernet std I/O parallel port tablet mouse HPS communications 2 SSA enhanced wide SCSI I/O
SAP DB Srvr/ main server	SP2 High Node 8 CPUs	2 Gb	2 – 2.2Gb SCSI 32 – 2.2Gb SSA 32 – 4.5Gb SSA	keyboard diskette std I/O parallel port 8-port async integrated Ethernet 3 high perf Ethernet HPS communications SSA enhanced wide SCSI I/O mouse
SAP DB Srvr/ main server BACKUP	SP2 High Node 8 CPUs	2 Gb	2 – 2.2Gb SCSI 32 – 2.2Gb SSA 32 – 4.5Gb SSA	keyboard diskette std I/O parallel port 8-port async integrated Ethernet 3 high perf Ethernet HPS communications SSA enhanced wide SCSI I/O mouse

SAP application servers	6 SP2 Super Thin Nodes 1 CPU each	512 Mb	2 – 2.2Gb SCSI	keyboard diskette std I/O parallel port integrated Ethernet 2 high perf Ethernet HPS communications SSA enhanced mouse
Lego Server	SP2 Thin Node 1 CPU	512 Mb	2 – 2.2Gb SCSI 1 – 4.5Gb SCSI	keyboard/tablet diskette 2 high perf Ethernet parallel port mouse HPS communications 2 SSA wide SCSI
ATLAS application server	SP2 Thin Node 1 CPU	256 Mb	2 – 2.2Gb SCSI 4 – 2.2Gb SSA	keyboard diskette integrated Ethernet high perf Ethernet HPS communications SSA enhanced mouse
CSLM, PES	SP2 Thin Node 1 CPU	256 Mb	2 – 2.2Gb SCSI 8 – 2.2Gb SSA	keyboard diskette 2 Ethernet parallel port HPS communications SSA enhanced mouse
AMPS server ANALYZER	SP2 Thin Node 1 CPU	512 Mb	2 – 2.2Gb SCSI 4 – 2.2Gb SSA 2 – 4.5Gb SSA	keyboard diskette 2 Ethernet parallel port HPS communications SSA enhanced mouse
NOB, MIKER, Secondary namesrvr	SP2 Thin Node 1 CPU	256 Mb	2 – 2.2Gb SCSI	keyboard diskette 2 Ethernet parallel port HPS communications SSA enhanced mouse
EURO/Sales Analyzer	SP2 Thin Node 1 CPU	512 Mb	2 – 2.2Gb SCSI 8 – 2.2Gb SSA	keyboard diskette 2 Ethernet parallel port HPS communications SSA enhanced mouse

ATLAS database server	SP2 Wide Node 1 CPU	512 Mb	2 – 2.2Gb SCSI 64 – 2.0Gb SSA 11 – 4.5Gb SSA	keyboard/tablet diskette 2 high perf Ethernet parallel port mouse HPS communications 2 SSA wide SCSI
Consumer Response System	Model 58H 1 CPU	256 Mb	2 – 2.2Gb SCSI 14 – 4.5Gb Raid Tower	keyboard diskette Ethernet parallel port tablet mouse 3 wide SCSI
QAD Production PVCS Secondary DNS	Model 980B 8 CPUs	384 Mb	4 – 1.07Gb Serial Link 4 – 2.0Gb Serial Link 4 – 2.0Gb MTI SCSI	Serial-Link disk diskette High Perf Ethernet parallel port FDDI primary card Wide SCSI I/O cont SSA Adapter
Control Workstations (2)	2 Model 39H 1 CPU ea.	128 Mb	2 – 2.2 Gb 8 – 4.5 Gb SSA	keyboard diskette parallel port 8-port async integrated Ethernet high perf Ethernet HPS communications SSA Enhanced wide SCSI I/O mouse GXT150M Graphics
Domain Name Server	F30	120 Mb	4 Gb	CD-ROM Tape drive (5.0 Gb)

Other Hardware:

Server	Memory	Details	Adapters
Alphaserver 8200 2 CPUs	1 Gb	5/300	KZPSA PCI-FWD SCSI KFTIA Integrated I/O PrestoServer I/O Cache 2 HSZ40B RAID Cont

Tape Drives:

Tape Model	Vendor	Number of	C.U. Model
EXB480	Exabyte	1	8MM
EXB3494	Exabyte	1	3590

Terminals Attached Locally:

CRT Model	Vendor	Number of
Async Pseudo Terminal	IBM	11

b. LAN

Processors:

	CPU Model	CPU	Vendor	Size	Special Features
Winframe/NT 3.51	Proliant – 128Mb	1	Compaq	14 Gb	
NT 3.51	5000 – 128 Mb	2	Compaq	1.96 Gb	
Citrix Winframe/ Entrprse 1.6/NT 3.51	5000R – 384 Mb Pentium Pro w/512	3 1	Compaq	5 – 4Gb	
NT 3.51/ ACE srvr 2.2/ACE clnt 4.0	Pentium 133 – 32Mb	1	Compaq	1 Gb	
	Compaq 5000 R/200 – dual Pentium pro w/256 Mb	2	Compaq	2 – 2.1 Gb 7 – 4.3 Gb	Ext SCSI storage Mod1 smart array 2P SCSI cntrl monitor keyboard
A cc:mail OS/2	486 Deskpro 66M 32Mb	1	Compaq	150 Mb	
C cc:mail OS/2 D cc:mail OS/2	486 Deskpro 33M 32Mb	2	Compaq	150 Mb Digi	
G cc:mail WIN/95	5150 32Mb	1	Compaq	2 – 1.2Gb	
Global cc:mail OS/2	5150 32Mb	1	Compaq	1.2 Gb	
Ntmd cc:mail WIN	5150 32Mb	1	Compaq	1.2 Gb	
Lotus Notes Windows NT 3.51	Proliant 5000 128Mb	2	Compaq	12 Gb	
Lotus Notes OS/2 3.0 Warp	9595-OMT 64Mb	1	IBM	4 Gb	
Lotus Notes Windows NT 3.51	Proliant 4500 SMP 98Mb	2	Compaq	12 Gb	

Other Hardware:

Model	Vendor	Number of	Description
Netblazer	Netblazer	3	

NOTE: The above information is based upon the assumption that the LAN in place at the recovery site is equivalent to a 10Mb switched line. Please outline existing capabilities related to this assumption.

c. Workstations

Processors:

CPU Model	Size	Number of
Minimum 486 – 8 Mb min.	640 Mb	150
NT Workstation – Pentium 133	2 Gb	12

2. Operating Systems Software

a. RS/6000 SP2
AIX 4.15

RS/6000
AIX 4.14

b. LAN
NT 3.51

c. Windows for Workgroups
Version 3.11

3. Communications

Dial-Up Lines:

Number of Dial lines	Modem specs
28	Telebit
32	Multitech MT2834

4. Communications Services:

Sprint – 2 T1 lines to the Frame Relay Network (4700 Cisco Rtrs)
– 1 T1 line to NYC
– 1 T1 line to Atlanta

5. Test Time

The vendor should provide test time for each contract year. Test time should be included in the proposed hot-site services.

ABCD should have the right to purchase additional test time on the hot-site configuration for the purposes of testing ABCD's business continuity plan. The additional test time should be scheduled in blocks of eight hours and should be scheduled in advance.

The vendor should provide a copy of their test scheduling policy.

II. PROPOSAL PREPARATION/SUBMISSION

A. Questions

All questions regarding this RFP are to be addressed to:

Mr. John E. Smith
Director, IT Infrastructure
ABCD Company
123 Main Street
Chicago, IL 60601   (555) 555–1234

B. Delivery of Proposals

All proposals are to be submitted in triplicate (three copies). One copy should be delivered to the above address.

The other copies should be delivered to:

Mr. Tom X. Jones
Director,
Information Technology Infrastructure
ABCD Company
678 E Street
Chicago, IL 60601

C. Acceptance or Rejection of Proposal

ABCD reserves the sole right to decide whether a proposal does or does not substantially comply with the requirements of this RFP, and to accept, reject or negotiate modifications to vendor proposals or parts thereof. The lowest bidder will not necessarily be awarded the contract.

All proposals submitted will be considered proprietary and will not be released to any outside party in part or in full. Neither the transmission of the RFP to a prospective vendor nor acceptance of a reply shall imply any obligation or commitment on the part of ABCD.

D. Contract Award

Vendors will be notified of the acceptance or non-acceptance of their proposals by letter.

E. Timeframe

This RFP is only being submitted to hot-site vendors. It is intended that the selection of a site will be followed by the finalization of a formalized business continuity plan. To achieve this, we have set the following timetable:

RFP Issued	3/11/01
Deadline for Proposals	3/24/01
Supplier Selection	4/15/01

III. VENDOR INSTRUCTIONS

A. General Instructions on Proposal Format

To simplify the evaluation and selection process, the submitted proposal must be prepared following the order of Section IV, Technical Specifications and Requirements. ABCD's evaluation process incorporates the placing of a weighted point value upon each item of information specifically requested in this RFP. Failure to complete and follow the response format in the required sequence, even if addressed elsewhere in the proposal document, may result in diminished value being accorded to a vendor's response.

B. Special Instructions

1. Services

The vendor shall provide both hot-site and work area site services. The vendor shall provide access to the work area site and hot-site within two hours after notification. Following a declared disaster, ABCD shall be permitted to occupy the hot-site and work area site for a period up to six weeks and the cold site facility for a period of up to twelve months.

2. Contract Term

The vendor shall provide pricing for 1, 3, and 5 year term(s).

3. Vendor Contract

This RFP and the successful vendor's response will be part of the final agreement. Vendors should bear this in mind, and should not include any items in their proposal which they are not prepared to include in a contract.

4. Price Guarantee

Vendors must guarantee, within the response, that all cost information provided shall be valid for a period of 120 days.

5. Authorized Signature

The vendor's proposal must represent that it has been executed by an individual authorized to legally bind the vendor.

6. Exceptions

Each proposal shall clearly identify any exceptions to the mandatory requirements, explain each exception and describe any recommended alternatives. Failure to clearly identify any exception to any mandatory requirement will constitute a representation by the vendor that it will fulfill the mandatory requirement for no cost in addition to those set forth in the vendor's proposal.

7. Proposed Recovery Configuration

Any hardware or communications equipment proposed by the vendor which is not currently installed and operational shall be clearly identified. By proposing such equipment, the vendor agrees to have the equipment installed and operational within 30 days of contract award.

The vendor shall identify the number of alternate recovery sites which are capable of ABCD's configuration as provided in this RFP. The vendor shall identify the proposed sites as primary or alternate. If sites are not dedicated to recovery, they should be specifically called out.

8. Prime Contractor

Please identify any part of the services described in your response which are not provided entirely by your company. Please provide full operational documentation for any business partner and identify and explain any differences. Explain the rationale for proposing a partner versus a single source location.

9. Single Site/Single Source

Please identify how every site involved in your solution is configured and staffed. Explain how multiple sites will be coordinated. Explain, in detail, how the network will be recovered and managed.

IV. TECHNICAL SPECIFICATIONS AND REQUIREMENTS

Specific information concerning the services and facilities being proposed by the vendor is contained in this section of the RFP.

The vendor's proposal must respond to each point, whether the vendor can or cannot meet the requirement. If any requirement cannot be met, a full explanation must be given, and, if appropriate, an alternate proposal made.

The vendor is also required to respond first to the following items contained under RFP section III, Vendor Instructions:

Item 7, Proposed Recovery Configuration
Item 8, Prime Contractor
Item 9, Single Site/Single Source

A. Vendor Profile

1. Vendor Corporate Profile

This section must provide a brief overview of the vendor's company and services, including discussion of:

History
Customer Service Approach
Organizational and Corporate Synergy
Prior 12 Months' Investment into Business Continuity Services
Mission Statement

2. Local Vendor Support

Please provide a brief overview of where the support of ABCD will originate and list any facilities owned or operated by your company within 100 miles. List support available before a disaster, during a disaster, while operating at the hot-site and work area site and while operating at the cold site.

3. Experience
   a. How many customer declarations has the vendor supported to date?
   b. How many non-customer declarations has the vendor supported to date?
   c. How many customer declarations has the vendor supported to date where the recovered configuration was equal to or greater than ABCD's required configuration?
   d. How many successful customer tests has the vendor supported to date?

4. References
The vendor must provide three references of customers currently under subscription for a recovery configuration equal to or greater than ABCD's requirements. The references must include at least one customer who has used the vendor's services to recover from an actual disaster; the remainder should have conducted at least one test.

5. Financial Data
This section should contain information describing the current financial condition of the vendor's company. Include the latest annual report.

B. Subscriber Data
   1. At present, how many subscribers does the vendor support?
   2. How many of these subscribers have a recovery configuration equal to or greater than that of ABCD?
   3. How many of these subscribers utilize the same primary recovery facility as being proposed to ABCD?
   4. How many of these subscribers which utilize the same primary recovery facility as being proposed to ABCD are within a 50 mile radius of ABCD's facility?

C. Vendor Policies

1. Subscriber Risk Limitations
   a. How does the vendor limit the number of subscribers allowed per facility?
   b. Will the vendor contractually agree to limit the number of subscribers?
   c. How does the vendor plan to manage the risk of simultaneous declarations from multiple subscribers of the same configuration size as ABCD?
   d. How does the vendor assure that frivolous disaster declarations are not made?

2. Vendor Integrity
   a. Will the vendor allow a non-subscriber to declare and subsequently recover at the vendor's recovery facility?
   b. If yes, provide details of the recovery.
   c. If no, does the vendor contractually agree to not grant access to non-subscribers for the purposes of testing or business continuity?

3. **Sharing of Recovery Facility**
   a. What is the vendor's policy on handling the recovery of multiple sub-scribers when both are using the same recovery hardware, i.e. CPU sharing?
   b. Does the vendor allow sharing by more than one subscriber at the same recovery facility? If yes, how will the vendor protect the confidentiality of ABCD's data?

4. **Preemptive Access Rights**
   Will the vendor allow any subscriber to have preemptive access rights over ABCD? If yes, please describe the circumstances.

5. **Multiple/Regional Disaster Support**
   a. What is the vendor's policy on regional disasters or multiple, simultaneous disasters when more than one subscriber invokes a disaster declaration?
   b. Can the vendor provide access to additional hardware at the time of the disaster? What rights to access are granted to ABCD?
   c. If ABCD is required to access a facility other than the primary recovery facility, how will ABCD's telecommunications requirements be supported?

6. **Disaster Alert and Declaration**
   a. Define the vendor's disaster alert and declaration procedure.
   b. Does the vendor require a fee be paid when placing a disaster declaration or alert?
   c. Does the vendor require subscribers to place a disaster declaration in order to "reserve" a recovery facility?
   d. How does the vendor assign a recovery facility when a subscriber places a disaster declaration?

7. **Disaster Avoidance**
   What is the vendor's methodology and capability to provide disaster avoid-ance support? Provide examples of proactive involvement by the vendor to avert customer disasters.

8. **Internal Business Continuity Plan**
   Attach a copy of the vendor's plan to respond to a disaster occurring at the proposed recovery site.

9. **Testing Methodology and Support**
   a. Provide a summary of the vendor's testing methodology and standard support provided during tests.
   b. What type of support does the vendor provide before, during and after a test? What type of fee is associated with this support?
   c. Does the vendor support remote testing?

    d. Does the vendor provide turnkey testing services? If yes, detail the extent of services provided.

    e. What additional fees will the subscriber incur during testing (i.e. telephone expense, etc.)?

10. Facility Audit

Will the vendor allow a representative of ABCD or an independent third party not under contract with the vendor to audit the proposed recovery facility?

11. Internal Quality Program

Describe the vendor's internal service quality control and continuous improvement program.

12. Vendor Commitment

    a. How much investment has the vendor made in technology in the past 12 months?

    b. What is the vendor's policy for providing services for new technologies?

    c. Has the vendor ever closed a recovery facility? Please provide the details, including the customers' ramifications surrounding the closures.

    d. How much investment in technology does the vendor plan on making in the next 12 months?

D. Recovery Facility Specifications

1. Location(s) Available

    a. Provide a list of all the vendor's recovery facility location(s). Indicate the proposed primary and alternate facilities capable of supporting ABCD's required configuration. (Also refer to Item 7, Proposed Recovery Configuration, under Section III, Vendor Instructions.)

    b. Provide a list of all hot-site and work office site facilities. Indicate if the proposed hot-site is co-located with the primary work area site.

    c. Provide a summary of the vendor's local remote testing recovery facility and local work area (end user) recovery capability.

2. Telecommunications

    a. Describe the local telephone company and inter-exchange carrier access installed at your proposed recovery site suitable for recovering ABCD's network.

    Discuss the following:

        (1) Access methods, standard telephone company and alternate access vendors, if any

        (2) Capacity

        (3) Diversity

        (4) Carrier services available on a subscription basis

    b. Describe the above parameters at your alternate recovery site(s) in the event that the primary recovery site is not available.

    c. Describe how you can/will reroute ABCD's network and communications to the primary or alternate recovery site(s).

Describe the following:
(1) Use of standard carrier services
(2) Use of your dedicated business continuity network
d. Describe any pertinent network recovery expertise and capabilities.

3. Remote Testing
Please outline the vendor's capabilities for testing the primary configuration from ABCD's home site and/or any alternate site.

4. Facility Control
   a. Of the recovery facilities identified above, indicate which ones are owned by the vendor, which ones are leased by the vendor and which ones are multi-tenant.
   b. If multi-tenant, what are the zoning codes for the area in which the facility is located?
   c. Identify any tenants that may be located within the vendor's recovery facility and the nature of their business.
   d. If any recovery facility is utilized for anything else besides business continuity, indicate the location of the recovery facility and its use.

5. Access/Occupancy
   a. ABCD requires immediate access after a disaster declaration.
   b. ABCD requires a minimum of 4 weeks of occupancy in the hot-site following a disaster declaration.

6. Fire Detection/Suppression System
Detail the fire detection and suppression system of the proposed recovery facility.

7. Security System
Detail the security system and security staff provided at the proposed recovery facility. Identify any logical security software which ABCD will be required to run under. If the customer can use their own security software, please note this.

8. Environmental Equipment
Detail the environmental support equipment of the proposed recovery facility:

   a. Power Conditioning
   b. HVAC
   c. Chiller
   d. UPS
   e. Diesel Generator

Indicate whether the proposed recovery facility has redundant capabilities for the above environmental support equipment.

9. **Utility Vendors**
   a. Detail which utility (electrical and communications) vendors service the proposed recovery facility.
   b. Indicate redundant capabilities for electrical and communications utilities in the event of an outage.

10. **Customer Equipment**
    Describe the provision for the subscriber's placement of critical equipment at the recovery facility.

11. **Maintenance Procedures**
    What are the maintenance procedures for the recovery facility, hardware and environmental support equipment at the proposed recovery facility?

12. **Geographical Location**
    What is the geographical location (i.e. urban or suburban) of the proposed recovery facility and its proximity to a local airport?

13. **Transportation**
    Provide details regarding the number of daily flights from ABCD's location to the proposed recovery facility; average flight time; and average commute from the local airport to the recovery facility.

14. **Lodging/Restaurants**
    How many hotels and restaurants are available within a 5-mile radius of the proposed recovery facility? Do the local area hotels offer corporate discounts to the vendor's customers?

15. **Backup Recovery Sites**
    Repeat information in items 6 through 14 for backup recovery sites.

E. **Recovery Configuration**
   The vendor shall detail the proposed hot-site and work area site recovery configuration as indicated below. The vendor shall provide a line-by-line comparison between the required recovery configuration detailed under Section I, Introduction, Paragraph C. Recovery Configuration Specifications and their proposed configuration. The vendor shall indicate the recovery configurations proposed for both the primary and alternate site(s) being proposed.

   If a specific requirement cannot be met, the vendor shall explain why and, if applicable, offer an alternate solution. The vendor shall also provide details regarding optional services available.

   This section of the proposal shall not contain any cost data. All cost data should be included under Paragraph F, Proposed Pricing.

1. **Hot-Site and Work Area Site**
   a. Hardware

    b. Operating System
    c. Communications
    d. Testing
    e. Work Space
    f. Office equipment (i.e. Copiers, fax machines, etc.)

2. Cold Site
    a. Location of Proposed Cold Site
    b. Square Footage

3. Optional Services
    a. Mobile Recovery Facility
    b. Other Optional Services

F. Proposed Pricing
The vendor shall provide pricing for 1-, 3- and 5-year term(s) for the proposed recovery configuration. The vendor shall also include pricing for all optional services proposed. Pricing shall include the monthly subscription fee, disaster declaration fee, daily usage fees, and any other associated fees (including one-time fees).

	1 Year	*3 Years*	*5 Years*

1. IBM RS/6000
a. Monthly Subscription
b. Disaster Declaration
c. Daily Usage
d. Optional Services
e. Associated Fees

2. LAN
a. Monthly Subscription
b. Disaster Declaration
c. Daily Usage
d. Optional Services
e. Associated Fees

3. Workstations
a. Monthly Subscription
b. Disaster Declaration
c. Daily Usage
d. Optional Services
e. Associated Fees

4. Work Area Site
a. Monthly Subscription
b. Disaster Declaration

   c. Daily Usage
   d. Optional Services
   e. Associated Fees

5. Any additional standard and/or incremental configuration charges related to this specific recovery installation

(Please specify below)

Fee
$ _____   _____   _____
$ _____   _____   _____
$ _____   _____   _____
$ _____   _____   _____
$ _____   _____   _____

6. Optional Services (Not Included Above)
Fee
$ _____   _____   _____
$ _____   _____   _____
$ _____   _____   _____
$ _____   _____   _____
$ _____   _____   _____

G. Staff and Services

1. Support Staff Availability
   a. Indicate the number of support staff personnel (and their position) on site during testing and business continuity.
   b. Indicate the amount of experience your support staff has as it relates to testing and business continuity.

2. Support Area
Describe the support area available with a hot-site and cold site subscription for ABCD personnel. Is this area shared with other subscribers?

3. Work Area
Describe what support facilities, including office space and equipment (FAX, photocopying, microcomputers, voice communications, desks, chairs, terminals, etc.), are provided for ongoing user assistance.

4. Support Services
Describe what types of support services the vendor provides as part of this contract and what types of support services are available at an additional fee.

5. Replacement Equipment Services
Describe the vendor's capability to provide expedited replacement equipment for the ABCD's home configuration.

6. Professional Services
Describe your range of available professional services to assist us with:

Corporate Planning
Business Impact Analysis
BCP Development
Other

Please include any automated business continuity planning tools which are supported by the vendor, and which can be made available to ABCD.

H. Terms and Conditions

1.   Priority Access
a.   Provide the vendor's policy for preempting ABCD's right of access to the primary recovery configuration by another subscriber.
b.   In the event of a multiple disaster will resources be shared or limited to ABCD?

2.   Upgrades
Provide the vendor's provisions for upgrading ABCD's recovery configuration during the term of the contract.

3.   Automatic Renewal
a.   What is the length of term of the automatic renewal?
b.   How much notice does the vendor customarily provide if it is not going to renew?

Describe the vendor's policy regarding annual price escalation.

I.   Additional Information
The vendor should include any additional information that they feel would aid ABCD in their review process. This information should be limited to information the vendor feels is pertinent to this response which was not specifically asked for in the RFP (i.e. marketing structure, additional support provided, optional services, etc.). The vendor should be selective in the material to be included in this section.

The above is an example of the types of things that should be included in an RFP. However, this should give you a better understanding of the categories of information that should be included.

Once the vendors respond to the RFP, a decision matrix can be designed and used to determine the most cost-effective option.

Hot-Site with Electronic Vaulting

Electronic vaulting means that data are backed up, and the output is electronically transmitted to an intermediate location or to a hot-site for storage. One method of accomplishing this is to use stand-alone tape drives that receive and write data to removable tapes, which may be stored in racks or bins. Another method of electronic vaulting would be to incorporate an automated tape library, virtual tape library or direct access storage device.

In electronic vaulting, there is a logical backup process which is staged to direct access, or to tape prior to transmission. Organizations are more likely to achieve a shorter recovery time if the electronic vault is located at the alternate site or connected to the alternate site through channels capable of long distance connectivity and high bandwidth. Using this strategy, the amount of data loss can range from one day's worth to just a few minutes' worth.

Active Recovery Site (Mirrored)

This strategy involves two active sites, each capable of taking over the other's workload in the event of a disaster. Each site will have enough idle processing power to restore data from the other site and to accommodate the excess workload in the event of a disaster. The two sites should be physically removed from each other and should be at greater than campus-wide if they are to handle regional disasters, such as floods or hurricanes.

This strategy maintains selected data such that both copies of the data (local and remote copies) are synchronized. This requires that updates to data be received at both the primary and secondary locations before the owning application is notified that the update is complete. This requires dedicated hardware at both sites, with the capability to automatically transfer the workload between sites.

Using this strategy, virtually no data will be lost in the event of a disaster, thus providing for continuous availability. In a mainframe environment, achieving these capabilities requires control units capable of creating shadow copies of data and data synchronization, channel extenders, and channels with extended distance connection and high bandwidth. Achieving this strategy's objectives with distributed systems is not usually accomplished with channel extension technologies. Software-based solutions that send data over a shared network using a communication protocol such as TCP/IP are available for many distributed platforms.

Reciprocal Agreements

Another form of acquiring computer system redundancy is to enter into a reciprocal agreement with an organization with similar hardware and software. This strategy was popular in the 1970s and 1980s. Its attractive feature was that it represented a much lower cost than the hot-site option. Many organizations entered into such agreements and felt protected until the time came to actually use this backup source. The reason why this solution does not appear on the chart is that many organizations found that these agreements were not enforceable. The organizations that were being relied upon did not have the reserve computer capacity to service two organizations so their own organization's work took priority. The same is true when the time came to test the backup system: there was not enough capacity.

Reciprocal agreements sound like a good idea, but when needed, generally they are not effective. They should rarely be considered as a viable strategy.

OTHER COMPONENT RECOVERY

Many Business Continuity Planning consultants focus only on IT stategies when developing a plan. The point that they are missing is that an organization is dependent upon many components or resource categories to be functional. Each of these components must be examined for a single point of failure and a strategy must be developed to mitigate that risk. Figure 4.4 shows the conceptual model for a typical organization. If each component for each business unit within an organization is addressed and accounted for in the BCP, then the plan should prove successful when called upon during an actual disaster.

COMMUNICATIONS RECOVERY

Recovering communications capabilities is critical to a vast number of organizations. Voice and data communications are vital links between an organization's business units and between itself and its vendor and customer base.

Voice Communications

Redundancy is quite important to protect both voice and data communications. Strategy considerations include the use of multiple carriers (MCI, AT&T, Sprint, etc.), multiple points of entry into the facility, and having the multiple lines coming from multiple Central Offices (COs).

There should be periodic backup of the programmable circuit board within the PBX system. The organization and the communications carrier should prearrange

- Customers
- Supply Chain Inputs
- Communications
  - Data
  - Voice
- Computers
  - Mainframe
  - Midrange
  - Servers
  - Personal Computers
- Software
- Data
  - Magnetic Media
  - Non-Magnetic Media
- Facilities
  - Electricity
    - Commercial
    - Emergency Generator
    - Battery
  - HVAC
  - Security Systems
  - Structure
- People
  - Skill Sets
  - Availability
  - Procedures
- Furniture
- Office Equipment
- Production Equipment
- Office Supplies

Figure 4.4 Conceptual component business model

a method of switching calls from one location to another. Finally, the organization should consider institutionalizing periodic updating of schematics or descriptions of circuitry and node identification and storing those off-site.

Voice communications with employees is also important during an emergency situation. Some organizations have an employee 1–800 number that allows the organization to leave a pre-recorded message so that employees can call and find out the status of the company and whether or not they should report to work. A few organizations have taken this one step further and allowed employees to leave messages on the 1–800 system. This is invaluable when you are trying to determine the status of *all* employees.

Data Communication

As with voice communications the Strategy considerations for data communications include the use of multiple carriers (MCI, AT&T, Sprint, etc.) and multiple points of entry into the facility. Additionally, there should be redundancy in the lines for the wide-area network. As with voice communications, there should be a schematic or description of the network.

FACILITIES RECOVERY

Structure

Strategies for the recovery of the physical plant are limited to having an empty facility ready to move into (not a good business decision), moving in with another business unit that has sufficient space (again, not efficient from a business perspective), or having an arrangement set up with a commercial real estate broker. In an area-wide disaster it is a case of excessive demand facing a limited supply. Those that have pre-arranged agreements with critical vendors win the game.

Power

Nearly a third of all disaster declarations are caused by a lack of power. With this in mind, it is somewhat surprising that many strategies overlook this key component.

There are several ways to add redundancy to an organization's power requirements. The most common is to purchase an emergency electricity generator. The vendors of these generators will be happy to assess the power requirements of the organization and provide a generator that can accommodate electrical needs during an emergency. Many organizations have purchased emergency generators that will only power emergency lighting and the elevator systems. With a little tweaking by the vendor, those generators can be powered up to also handle computer systems. A word of caution about diesel generators: make sure that they are powered up and accept a full power load every month or so and that the diesel fuel is changed regularly. These two rituals will greatly enhance your chances of actually having emergency power when it is needed.

Another redundancy strategy is to create linkages to several power substations and have each of those linkages entering the facility at different locations. With aging electric utility infrastructures, this is a relatively inexpensive option in a major metropolitan environment.

A third redundancy strategy is to have the organization wired to accept an emergency generator hook-up. There are a number of vendors that have emergency diesel generators mounted on flatbed trucks that can go to a facility and supply power at short notice. In order to do this, the organization must first be wired to receive the power and understand ahead of time their power requirements.

INSURANCE

If the organization chooses not to adopt a recommended strategy, or if no other reasonable strategy is available, insurance coverage can be used as a strategy to keep the company financially viable. Unless you have an extensive insurance background, it is recommended that an insurance adjuster be contacted to assess (usually done without charge) the company's insurance coverage in light of your findings and evaluations to this point.

The necessity of insuring tangible assets like buildings, machinery and equipment is readily accepted by business owners and managers. What is not appreciated in all cases is the need for business income insurance to protect the business when a disabling loss occurs.

From a business perspective, the advantage of owning any asset is the right to its use and to the revenue it generates. If this revenue stream is not properly insured when a loss occurs, the results could be catastrophic to those having rights to the property. While it is proper that the value of the asset itself be insured, losing the ability to generate revenue could easily force an owner out of the business. A short example might make the point.

A title company's regional office suffered a fire loss set by a disgruntled employee (we didn't actually find out until he was caught trying the same thing at his next employer). Based on an estimate of direct asset loss, the title company was ready to settle for $400,000 with their insurance. The title company invited an insurance adjuster to see if what the insurance company was offering was a fair settlement. After an extensive assessment of all factors that would affect the company's equity, the adjuster countered the insurance company's offer with a claim for $2.3 million. A settlement was finally reached for $1.4 million. Even though the insurance adjuster received 10% of the final settlement, the title company ended up ahead financially.

Fortunately, this particular company, with due credits to their insurance broker, had purchased adequate business interruption insurance before the potentially devastating event occurred. Equally important, perhaps, the client sought outside professional assistance that proved to be critical when an impasse was reached with the carrier over the true value of the claim.

As an internal or external consultant it is important to understand enough about insurance so that you can recognize the need and request the assistance of the proper experts as required.

Business Income Insurance

Business income insurance (aka business interruption insurance) covers a company's loss in net profit due to a disaster. It also covers continuing expenses that a company is obligated to pay during the time the company is unable to operate.

It is important to note that business income insurance is a contingent coverage. That is, it covers consequential loss resulting from a direct loss to property. Thus a company's property must suffer a direct loss which is covered under that company's property policy. The consequential loss in profit and/or continuing expenses would be covered by business income insurance. If there is no direct loss to property, or that loss is not covered by the insured's property policy, then the business income insurance would not respond.

The application of business income insurance is obvious: it reimburses a company the revenue it normally generates while it is unable to do so. This increases the chance of quick successful recovery and retention of customers. A question that should be asked when purchasing this policy is: Is there a timeframe during which the policy will respond. For example, some policies will pay for losses up to only one year after the date of the disaster. Some policies will pay indefinitely, up to the purchased limit. This is an important consideration, as a company's full recovery to the level of operation before it suffered the disaster could take several years.

Additional Coverages

There are three items of additional coverage that can be applied to the basic business income coverage: extra expense, civil authority, and alterations and new buildings. Collectively, these additional coverages extend the basic business income coverage to provide the equivalent of the coverage of combined business interruption and extra expense in a simpler and somewhat broader fashion.

- *Extra Expense*—covers necessary expenses incurred during the period of restoration that would not have been incurred if the property loss that necessitated them had not occurred. This includes relocation expenses and costs to equip and operate a replacement or temporary location. This also covers the extra expense to repair or replace property and the extra expense to research, replace or restore the lost information on damaged records.

- *Civil authority*—covers loss caused by action of civil authority that prohibits access to the insured premises. This coverage applies for up to two consecutive weeks from the date of the action.
- *Alterations and new buildings*—extends the business income coverage to cover loss of business income sustained due to direct physical loss or damage at the described premises by any covered cause of loss to new buildings or structures, alterations or additions to existing buildings, and machinery, equipment, supplies or building materials located near the building and used in the construction of the new building.

STAFF RECOVERY

The contributions of staff are probably the most critical and important component of any business. Many planners who have not actually gone through a major disaster do not understand just how critical staff recovery can be. There must be sound strategies in place to ensure that staff contributions are recovered.

There must be a method of contacting and/or accounting for all staff members. Having a staff list by department is valuable immediately after a disaster so staff members can be counted for those forced outside the facility.

If the disaster occurs during non-working hours, a detailed list of staff members' telephone numbers and addresses should be used to assess staff status and to inform staff of the next steps. Notification can also be accomplished through radio and TV announcements.

As mentioned previously, some organizations have set up a 1–800 number to be used to notify staff members and to take messages. During an area-wide disaster, some staff may leave the area to find living accommodation elsewhere. This is an ideal method of allowing them to communicate to the organization where they have gone and their status.

For staff members who become unavailable, an agreement might be reached ahead of time for temporary borrowing of staff from other locations to fill staffing needs. As a final option, employment agencies will have to be contacted to replace missing staff. In either case, it is important to have employee job descriptions, or at least job titles, available when searching for replacements.

In general, employees will choose taking care of their children and finding shelter before they choose to go to their jobs. In a major area-wide disaster, daycare facilities and employee homes can be lost. In order to get employees back on the job, the organization may have to provide its own daycare facility and assist employees to find shelter for their families. One method of obtaining shelter for employees is to contact the organization's financial institution and request access to their repossessed housing inventory (REO for banks, OREO for savings and loans).

VENDOR SELECTION

The outside vendors that an organization must use are one of the most important elements of a recovery. Their goods and services must be relied upon to restore the productive capabilities of the organization. In an area-wide disaster, vendors must be contacted quickly so that replacement and repair can begin as soon as possible.

Several strategy considerations emanate from this vendor requirement. First, vendors should be contacted to determine if, in the event of a disaster, they would be able to supply the quantity and quality of goods or services required. The organization must determine where they would fall in the pecking order of all organizations to be serviced. The organization must establish an efficient means of contacting the vendor (emergency numbers, direct dial number to avoid unproductive voice-mail routing, etc.).

Second, if the organization uses the vendor on a regular basis, an arrangement should be made that in the event of a disaster, the organization would be one of the first to receive service.

Third, if the goods or service is vital to the organization, a second vendor outside a potential disaster area should be identified and contacted. For that matter, all vital goods and services should be represented by more than one vendor.

CUSTOMER RELATIONS

During a disaster situation an organization's goods and services will not be available to customers. In order to maintain market share, the customer base must be contacted and informed of the current situation. This can be done through the news media or by personal contact with customers.

In dealing with the news media, only designated staff should be allowed to discuss the disaster situation. A representative from the Public Relations staff or the CEO should be the only ones allowed to field questions from the press. If this strategy is not followed, it could have a devastating effect on future sales.

PLAN STRATEGIES

These are strategies relating to how the plan itself is structured. Strategies include the chain of command for the recovery, staffing of the recovery teams, how often to test the plan, and how the plan will be maintained.

The chain of command for the recovery should mirror the hierarchy of the organization. If this is not done, once the plan is executed the actual chain of command will take over the recovery and the plan will ultimately be deemed unusable.

Staff selection of the teams should be left to team leaders, and team leaders should be chosen relative to their position on the organizational hierarchy and their area of expertise. The Chief Information Officer, for instance, would be the ideal candidate to lead the Information Systems recovery team.

Testing and maintenance of the plan should be conducted at least once a year.

5 Plan Development

A BCP is an integrated set of procedures and resource information that is used to recover from an event that has caused a disruption to business operations. It answers the newspaper questions: who (who performs the recovery), what (what will be done), when (the ordering of procedures), where (where will the recovery take place) and how (what resources, vendors, and customers must be involved).

Upon the declaration of a disaster, the plan activates pre-approved policies and procedures. After a disaster, time is the enemy. If policies and procedures are established that are activated with the declaration of a disaster, precious time can be saved.

The plan restores the outflow of services with the least possible cost to the organization. The objective of the plan is to get the organization functional again. Before the disaster, the organization may have had expensive office furniture. For recovery purposes, flat surfaces and a place to sit will suffice. One of the objectives is to keep extraordinary expenses to a minimum.

The typical structure of a BCP addresses:

- initial response;
- damage assessment;
- employee notifications and mobilization; recovery team(s) roles, responsibilities, and procedures;
- employee, vendor and customer information; and
- test and maintenance procedures.

The logic of the plan design can be seen in Figure 5.1. The plan should be written to address a "worst-case" scenario. In so doing, lesser scenarios should also be covered. The plans should incorporate previously selected recovery strategies. Most importantly, the plan should be developed jointly with the client. If the client does not take ownership of the plan, it will probably not be used in a real emergency.

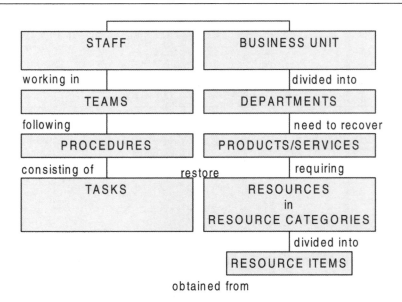

Figure 5.1 BCP design

An efficient method to help the client develop a plan is to create a "Straw-man" (Sample) plan and work with the client to modify the "Straw-man". If you give the client guidelines on procedure development and expect the plan to be put together with no further guidance, the project will either not be completed or will fall behind schedule. The Action Plan that will be presented later in this chapter is an ideal template to use in going through the "Straw-man" exercise.

TEAMS

The team structure is important to the recovery effort. Each team should be assigned tasks that are aligned with team member skill sets. During a recovery effort, their tasks relating to recovery should be their only concern. If team members are expected to perform recovery efforts and do their normal jobs, neither function will be done effectively. The key to success is focus.

The typical structure of teams is as shown in Figure 5.2. This structure may be contracted or expanded to meet a particular organization's needs. It is important to let the organization's Organization Chart guide the design of the team structure. Once the structure is developed, it should be presented to the CEO or other senior

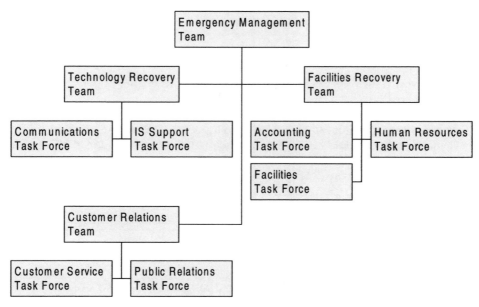

Figure 5.2   Typical structure of teams

executive for concurrence or modification. This executive will also designate the staff that will lead each of the teams.

The team leaders should then be contacted to determine who will be on the teams (in priority order) and who will be in charge of the various task forces. Likewise, the task force leaders will be asked to assemble their teams. Each team will have its members listed in order so that if the team leader is not available, the next person appearing on the team list will become the team leader. Obviously, when choosing the ordering of team members, you must continually assess whether or not the remaining team members would follow this team leader's directions during an emergency situation. If not, the plan will not work.

Emergency Management Team (EMT)

The Emergency Management team is responsible for ensuring the safety of staff during an emergency (evacuations, head counts, injury notification), for the declaration of a disaster situation, for assembling of the recovery teams, and for the monitoring and coordination of the recovery effort. To be effective, this team should comprise the most senior executives of the organization with the EMT manager being the CEO. Initially, the CEO will say that some other executive should handle this function. You should ask the CEO the following questions:

- In the event of a disaster, would you want to be kept informed of the progress of the recovery?
- Would you want to be in a position to make decisions regarding recovery priorities?
- Would you want your direct report staff members in charge of the components of the recovery?

If the answer to these questions is yes, then the CEO is doing the functions of the EMT manager and should be written into the plan. Otherwise, the plan will not be effective in a real disaster.

The Action Plan for the EMT should look something like the following:

Steps	Activities/actions/tasks	Additional information
1.	Potential disaster scenario emerges. Render aid to injured as needed (see "Emergency Procedures").	Initial observer
2.	Contact Business Continuity Coordinator (NAME) or any member of Senior Management.	Initial observer/Facilities Security Director
3.	Determine preliminary cause of disruption, if possible.	Initial observer, Senior Management, or Business Continuity Coordinator (if on the scene)
4.	Determine if facility evacuation is required. If evacuation is required, evacuate building. Assemble staff in breezeway/walk-through on the east side of the building across the street.	Senior Management or Business Continuity Coordinator
5.	Determine if casualties/injuries have occurred and contact the appropriate emergency services, as needed (see "Emergency Procedures").	Initial observer, Senior Management, or Business Continuity Coordinator (if on the scene)
6.	Administer First Aid/CPR, if required (see "Emergency Procedures").	Trained First Aid/CPR personnel
7.	Use staff listing and ensure that all staff have evacuated building.	EMT designated personnel
8.	Notify EMT members. Inform EMT members of potential disaster scenario. Inform EMT members to bring their BCP plan. Instruct EMT members to begin damage assessment.	Business Continuity Coordinator

Emergency Management Team

Team Functions:
- Identify disaster condition
- Identify recovery center
- Assemble team leaders and teams
- Monitor/record/manage the progress of the recovery

Alternate Site: Recovery Center

Team Succession List

The first person on the list is the EMT Manager. If that person is not available, the second person becomes the EMT Manager, and so on.

	First Name	Last Name	Home phone	Mobile phone	Beeper
01	ROBERT	LOWE			
02	ANDREW	KOSS			
03	PAUL	JELLY			
04	STEVEN	RANDINSKY			
05	JAMES	BLAKE			
	CHRISTOPHER	ROWE			
	Business Continuity Administrator				

Steps	Activities/actions/tasks	Additional information
9.	Notify families of injured staff.	EMT designated personnel. Use Recovery team member(s) who are HR specialists
10.	Alert team leaders of situation and request they remain available	EMT Team leaders can be found by examining the Technical Recovery Team, Facilities Recovery Team, or the Order Processing Team listings. The first person on the list is the team leader. If that person is not available, the second person becomes the team leader, and so on
11.	Begin damage assessment.	EMT This is a preliminary assessment. An in-depth assessment will be made during each procedure performed by the recovery teams

Steps	Activities/actions/tasks	Additional information
12.	Complete initial damage assessment.	EMT
13.	Document damage assessment.	EMT. Use EMT Event Log
14.	Determine (from report) if outage will exceed an "acceptable outage duration".	EMT Refer to the "BIA Duration Assessment" in the "Resource Item Matrix". If the functions that are damaged are expected to be non-functional for a period greater than the number of days listed, then the "acceptable outage duration" has been exceeded
15.	If outage is expected to be over an "acceptable" duration, declare a disaster. If less, communicate resumption of normal business operations and timeframe(s) involved.	EMT Manager
16.	Disaster Declared, notify all appropriate teams.	EMT
17.	Document all activities. Maintain "EMT Event Log".	EMT
18.	Based on Damage Assessment Report, determine if full (or partial) relocation to alternate sites is necessary.	EMT decision based on assessment of Office Recovery Team during "Recover Facilities" procedure
19.	Arrange for appropriate security controls to protect the facility.	Office Recovery Team, Facilities Security Specialist
20.	Address the news media if appropriate	EMT, Public Relations Specialist
21.	Brief all team leaders and team members to meet at recovery center if required.	EMT See "Recovery Center"
22.	Notify teams of plan activation.	Team leaders
23.	Continue to update media regarding the return of the organization to production mode.	EMT, Public Relations Specialist
24.	Monitor the progress of the plan.	EMT Manager. Use the team plan to check off completed tasks and procedures. Use the "EMT Event Log" to record events during the disaster and recovery efforts.

Emergency Management Team Event Log

Date/time	Event/situation	Action taken	Person(s) involved

The EMT procedures contain several key elements. As with all the other procedures, there is a column for Additional Information. This identifies who is to perform a task, which vendor to use, and amplifications of the task.

Within the procedure there is a task referring to dealings with the news media. Only the CEO or a designated staff member should be allowed to deal with the media.

At the end of the procedure is the "Event Log". For legal and insurance purposes, it is important that this log reflects the sequence of events of the entire disaster recovery effort.

Recovery Teams

The recovery teams should be made up of staff that are involved with the area being recovered. IT staff should be assigned to IT recovery teams and facilities staff should be assigned to the facilities recovery teams. Below is an example of an Action Plan involving both technical and non-technical teams:

ACTION PLAN BY TEAM

The Action Plan by Team is the primary report that will be used by recovery team members to restore resources. The plan is organized by Resource Category Restoration Procedure based upon a logical restoration sequence. Each restoration procedure will list tasks that are to be executed in order.

To the right of many tasks are vendors' names and phone numbers, qualification requirements for the team member that will be performing the task, or other useful information.

Some procedures are linked to a default vendor. These vendors will be listed to the right of the procedure title. A default vendor may be called on for all vendor-related tasks contained in the procedure. However, some of the tasks may be linked with specific vendors. For those specific tasks, the exception vendor should be used.

The team leader (the first person available on the team list) should delegate the responsibilities in the action plan to different team members. The team member should execute the plan in the order presented. If one task in the plan cannot be completed, continue with the next task and return to the skipped task as soon as possible. Remember, of course, that it is not necessary to restore resources that are not lost. If a procedure, task, or step is deemed to be "Not Applicable", move to the next procedure, task, or step.

The "Action Plan by Team" report is designed to minimize references to other reports; however, some references may still be necessary:

- If you cannot reach the primary contact for a vendor then refer to the "Detail Vendor List" for addresses, additional phone numbers, and secondary contacts.
- The "Action Plan by Team" is organized in order of resource restoration priority. One of the complications of this organization is that you may call a vendor for one item, then find later on that you must call the same vendor again for another item.
- For some resources such as Office Supplies, it does not make sense to assign a separate task for each item. For example, you would not have one task to get pencils and another to get pens. The task might simply say to get Office Supplies. In that case you need to refer to "Supplies". This report will list the resources, quantities, and sources.

Services Priority Order **(may be used for allocating scarce resources)**

- Data/Telecomm/IS Facilities
- IS Operations
- IS Support Services
- Market Structure
- Marketing/Public Relations

- Customer Service & Systems Support
- Market Regulation
- Market Regulation/Surveillance
- Listing
- Application Development
- Accounting Services
- Facilities
- Human Resources
- Facilities Security
- Legal and Office of the Secretary
- National Sales

Technical Recovery Team

Team Contact Sheet

Team Functions:	Coordinate recovery operations for Computers, Telecommunications, and Data Communications
Alternate Site:	Recovery Center

Technical Recovery Team Succession List

The first person on the list is the team/task force leader. If that person is not available, the second person becomes the team/task force leader, and so on.

First Name	Last Name	Home Phone	Mobile Phone	Beeper
STEVEN	RAND			
CHRISTOPHER	BROTHERS			
KRYSTYNA	JOBS			

Communications Task Force

First Name	Last Name	Home Phone	Mobile Phone	Beeper	Specialty
JOHN	KAVE				
TASKER	BUSH				
JEFFERY	WES				
JAMES	WILL				
RICHARD	STREY				

IS Support Task Force

First Name	Last Name	Home Phone	Mobile Phone	Beeper	Specialty
ASHOK	BHO				

MICHAEL	BONK
DAVID	CODE
JAMES	DEA
ROBERT	GUTIE
RANDY	HAR
KRYSTYNA	JOBS
LAWRENCE	KOS
CHRISTOPHER	LOTTE
PHIL	LOG
STEVEN	SMOTHERS
JOHN	WEBB

Recover Telecommunications

	Procedure	Communications Task Force. Task force members may call on the services of other IT personnel who are not members of the recovery team.
1.	*Damage assessment* • Make an assessment of the damage and replacement needs using the "Resource Item Matrix" report and the appropriate appendix. • Compile a report of missing or damaged items that need to be replaced or repaired. • Relay findings to the EMT. • Salvage and safeguard as many resources items as possible.	
2.	*Location determination* If the facility will never be reoccupied, go to "Plan Telephone Locations". Otherwise, proceed to next task.	
3.	*Direct line telephone* • Determine if telephone outage is due to power failure. • If outage is due to power failure, use direct line telephones for incoming and outgoing calls. Direct line access may found in the Switch Room.	
4.	*Damage mitigation* • If equipment is or has been exposed to moisture, remove it from electrical power sources (main power, electrical generator, UPS). • If the environment is contaminated, remove equipment and electromagnetic media to a controlled environment free from smoke, soot, water, and high humidity.	**Vendor Name** **Telephone Number** **Contact Name**

	• Prior to removal, label equipment to identify its home location and any other equipment to which it was connected. • Wipe off all moisture from outside electromagnetic media (diskettes, tapes, CDs). • Obtain written consent of manufacturer and vendors for the disaster procedures being taken on equipment under warranty or maintenance contract. • Do not allow vendors/staff to test, evaluate or diagnose damage prior to restoration. • Let the vendor de-install, re-install, then re-certify equipment. • Move damaged equipment into storage until an adjuster can look at it. • Prior to re-installation, ensure that surge protectors have remained functional.	
5.	*Recover telephones/voice lines* • Contact vendor for telephones and voice lines. • Request quantity of telephones and direct lines needed. • Request installation of new PBX systems if required. • Determine time of delivery and installation. • Monitor installation of PBX equipment.	**Vendor Name** **Telephone Number** **Contact Name**
6.	*Plan telephone locations* If telephones and/or the entire telephone system need to be installed or re-installed: • Determine the number of telephones and telephone lines needed. • Identify where telephones are to be located. • Determine if there are existing phone jacks near telephone installation sites. • Create blueprint/floor plan of facility. • On blueprint or floor plan, identify where new telephone jacks and telephones are to be installed. • Give a copy of blueprint/floor plan to the person who will be dealing with the vendor. • Monitor the delivery and installation of the telephone system.	
7.	*Forward phone service* If required to move to a temporary location: • Notify vendor and request that phone service (voice and fax) be forwarded to temporary location.	**Vendor Name** **Telephone Number** **Contact Name**
8.	Report status and actions taken to the Technology Recovery Team Leader who, in turn, will notify the EMT.	

Recover Mid-Range Computers

Procedure	IS Support Task Force. Task force members may call on the services of other IT personnel who are not members of the recovery team.
1. *Damage assessment* • Make an assessment of the damage and replacement needs using the "Resource Item Matrix" report and appropriate appendices. • Compile a report of missing or damaged items that need to be replaced or repaired. • Salvage and safeguard as many resources items as possible.	Record findings on the "Damage Assessment Form" at the end of the Technical Recovery team's procedures.
2. *Determine cause of outage* • Determine damage to equipment. • Determine if CPU is operational. • Determine if electricity is getting to CPU. • Determine if workstations are operational. • Check circuit breakers.	
3. *Damage mitigation* If equipment is or has been exposed to moisture, remove it from electrical power sources (main power, electrical generator, UPS). • If the environment is contaminated, remove equipment and electromagnetic media to a controlled environment free from smoke, soot, water and high humidity. • Prior to removal, label equipment to identify its home location and any other equipment to which it was connected. • Wipe off all moisture from outside electromagnetic media (diskettes, tapes, CDs). • Obtain written consent of manufacturer and vendors for the disaster procedures being taken on equipment under warranty or maintenance contract. • Do not allow vendors/staff to test, evaluate or diagnose damage prior to restoration. • Let the vendor de-install, re-install, then re-certify equipment. • Move damaged equipment into storage until an adjuster can look at it. • Prior to re-installation, ensure that surge protectors have remained functional.	**Vendor Name** **Telephone Number** **Contact Name**

4.	*Order replacement equipment* If mid-range computer equipment is damaged and requires replacement: • Contact vendor to configure and order new/used mid-range computer equipment to replace damaged equipment. Indicate to the vendor that this is an emergency situation and request the vendor's quickest possible response time. • Get a commitment on the delivery schedule for all new equipment. • Coordinate the installation of the new/used equipment with the Facilities Maintenance Coordinator and with the manufacturer's technical representative who will be installing the system. • Follow up on equipment ordered and status of the order.	**Vendor Name** **Telephone Number** **Contact Name**
5.	*Move to alternate location* If damage to the facility is such that all functions must relocate, move functional mid-range computers to an alternate site. Verify the following cabling requirements at alternate site: • 10 base T (Cat 5) or shielded twisted pair cabling. • RJ45 data connections. • Star coupler cabling and all necessary cabling for clusters. • Level 3 cabling to support printers (via RJ11 connectors). (If the above requirements are not present in the new facility, call cabling vendor and arrange to have above requirements met.) • Notify moving vendor of the need to move the mid-range computers from current site to the alternate site. • Install equipment and cabling as vendors become available. • Notify all internal customers of the new location and node number. Give internal customers an estimate of when you expect to be operational.	 **Vendor Name** **Telephone Number** **Contact Name**
6.	*Obtain installation assistance* If the mid-range computers require re-installation at the current site or at a new site: • Contact the equipment's manufacturer or other vendor certified for installation. • Request that the equipment be installed at the specified site as soon as the equipment is available for the procedure. • Notify vendor as soon as equipment is available.	 **Vendor Name** **Telephone Number** **Contact Name**

7.	*Install mid-range computer system* If new mid-range computers are being installed, or the old system is being re-installed: ● Retrieve system, program, and data backup tapes from off-site storage facility. ● Make backup of data tapes. ● Load system, program, and data tapes with the assistance of the installation vendor. ● Verify the integrity of the system. ● Connect to the communications network. ● Verify the integrity of the system at all satellite locations. ● Provide Accounting with a list of all new equipment, locations, and serial numbers.	**Vendor Name** **Telephone Number** **Contact Name** Accounting Task Force
8.	*Return to permanent facility* After the permanent facility is available to be re-occupied: ● Notify the communications and system installation vendors that they will be required for a move back to the permanent facility. ● Schedule preparatory work around a weekend move back to the permanent facility. ● Before equipment is moved back to the permanent facility, ensure that the system, programs, and data are backed up and safely stored off-site. ● Cease operations at the temporary facility. ● Return to the permanent facility. ● Re-install the system and attach communications network. ● Verify the integrity of the system both at the new facility and at the satellite facilities serviced by the mid-range computers.	**Vendor Name** **Telephone Number** **Contact Name**
9.	Report status and actions taken to the Technology Recovery Team Leader who, in turn, will notify the EMT.	

Recover Local Area Network and Servers

Procedure	IS Support Task Force. Task force members may call on the services of other IT personnel who are not members of the recovery team.
1. *Assess damage to LAN and servers* If a disaster has occurred and/or the LAN system and Servers have been affected: • Assess the damage to all network and server components including cables, boards, fileserver, workstations and printers and network equipment. • Make a list of all items to be repaired or replaced. • Select appropriate vendors from the "Vendor Detail" report. • Relay findings to the EMT.	Record findings on the "Damage Assessment Form" at the end of the Technical Recovery team's procedures. **Vendor Name** **Telephone Number** **Contact Name**
2. *Damage mitigation* If equipment is or has been exposed to moisture, remove it from electrical power sources (main power, electrical generator, UPS). • If the environment is contaminated, remove equipment and electromagnetic media to a controlled environment free from smoke, soot, water, and high humidity. • Prior to removal, label equipment to identify its home location and any other equipment to which it was connected. • Wipe off all moisture from outside of electromagnetic media (diskettes, tapes, CDs). • Obtain written consent of manufacturer and vendors for the disaster procedures being taken on equipment under warranty or maintenance contract. • Do not allow vendors/staff to test, evaluate or diagnose damage prior to restoration. • Let the vendor de-install, re-install, then re-certify equipment. • Move damaged equipment into storage until an adjuster can look at it. • Prior to re-installation, ensure that surge protectors have remained functional.	**Vendor Name** **Telephone Number** **Contact Name**
3. *Recover equipment* If LAN and server equipment is damaged and requires replacement: • Contact vendor to order new/used equipment to replace damaged equipment. Indicate to the vendor that this is an emergency situation and request the vendor's quickest possible response time.	**Vendor Name** **Telephone Number** **Contact Name**

	• Ensure that the tape backup system that will be used to restore the LAN server is compatible with the format of the backup tapes. • Get a commitment on the delivery schedule for all new or used equipment. • Coordinate the installation of the new/used equipment with the Asset Manager. • Follow up on equipment ordered and status of the order.	
4.	*Install LAN communications network and servers* If a new LAN or server needs to be installed, or if the existing network or servers need to be activated: • Contact the appropriate vendors and request assistance. • Retrieve/develop the schematic of the current LAN to assist the vendor in the creation of the new network or in the re-establishment of the old network. • Tell the vendor the time when the equipment is expected to be operational. • The Communications Task Force Leader/NT Network Director will tell the vendor the anticipated location of the equipment. • Determine when the vendor can commence the installation of the LAN. • Monitor the progress of the vendor.	**Communications Task Force** **Vendor Name** **Telephone Number** **Contact Name**
5.	*Replace software* • Determine requirements for replacement software. • Retrieve the original or backup copy of the software from the storage facility. • Obtain replacement software from vendor. • Load software. • Verify the operation of the replacement software.	**Vendor Name** **Telephone Number** **Contact Name**
6.	*Recover backup tapes* If the servers are damaged and need to be replaced, or if the system is unable to access the hard drive: • Obtain backup tapes from off-site storage location. • If possible, make a backup tape of the backup tape and store the first copy in a safe location. • Deliver the copy of the backup to the facility housing the LAN and servers.	**Vendor Name** **Telephone Number** **Contact Name**
7.	*Install LAN and server system* If new LAN and server is being installed, or the old system is being re-installed: • Using backup tapes, load system, program, and data tapes to the servers.	

	<ul><li>Verify the integrity of the system.</li><li>Connect the communications network.</li><li>Verify the integrity of the system at all network workstations.</li><li>Provide accounting with a list of all new equipment, locations, and serial numbers.</li></ul>	
8.	Report status and actions taken to the Technology Recovery Team Leader who, in turn, will notify the EMT.	

Recover Wide Area Network

	Procedure	Communications Task Force. Task force members may call on the services of other IT personnel who are not members of the recovery team. **Vendor Name** **Telephone Number** **Contact Name**
1.	*Damage assessment* Make an assessment of the damage and replacement needs. Compile a report of missing or damaged items that need to be replaced or repaired.<ul><li>Salvage and safeguard as many resources items as possible.</li><li>Relay findings to the EMT.</li></ul>	Record findings on the "Damage Assessment Form" at the end of the Technical Recovery team's procedures.
2.	*Trouble-shoot data communication* Verify that the modems, routers, hubs, matrix switch, ISP, and T1s are operational or identify the problem.	
3.	*Repair communications network* If a new communications network needs to be installed, or if the existing network needs to be activated:<ul><li>Contact the appropriate vendors and request assistance.</li><li>Retrieve/create the schematic of the current communications network to assist the vendor in the creation of the new network or in the re-establishment of the old network.</li><li>Determine when the vendor can commence the installation of the communications network.</li><li>Monitor the progress of the vendor.</li></ul>	
4.	*Verify communications is back on line*<ul><li>Verify that the problem has been corrected.</li><li>Verify all lines.</li><li>Return to normal processing.</li></ul>	

5.	Report status and actions taken to the Technology Recovery Team Leader who, in turn, will notify the EMT.	

Recover Personal Computers

	Procedure	IS Support Task Force. Task force members may call on the services of other IT personnel who are not members of the recovery team.
1.	*Damage assessment* • Make an assessment of the damage and replacement needs using the appropriate appendix. • Compile a report of missing or damaged items that need to be replaced or repaired. • Salvage and safeguard as many resources items as possible. • Relay findings to the EMT.	Record findings on the "Damage Assessment Form" at the end of the Technical Recovery team's procedures.
2.	*Damage mitigation* If equipment is or has been exposed to moisture, remove it from electrical power sources (main power, electrical generator, UPS). • If the environment is contaminated, remove equipment and electromagnetic media to a controlled environment free from smoke, soot, water, and high humidity. • Prior to removal, label equipment to identify its home location and any other equipment to which it was connected. • Wipe off all moisture from outside of electromagnetic media (diskettes, tapes, CDs). • Obtain written consent of manufacturer and vendors for the disaster procedures being taken on equipment under warranty or maintenance contract. • Do not allow vendors/staff to test, evaluate or diagnose damage prior to restoration. • Let the vendor de-install, re-install, then re-certify equipment. • Move damaged equipment into storage until an adjuster can look at it. • Prior to re-installation, ensure that surge protectors have remained functional.	**Vendor Name** **Telephone Number** **Contact Name**

3.	*Order new Work Stations and Peripherals* • Assess existing equipment for repair, replacement or permanent reassignment. • If equipment is damaged, make arrangements with Help Desk or vendor to pick up and repair. • If Help Desk is making repair, ensure Help Desk acquires sufficient spare parts inventory. • Review Microcomputer Resource Requirements and order required equipment. • Get an estimated delivery date from the equipment vendor. • Notify users of estimated arrival date and time. • Monitor delivery of equipment.	**Vendor Name** **Telephone Number** **Contact Name**
4.	*Replace software* • Determine requirements for replacement software. • Contact other users within the organization to determine if an unaffected copy of the software exists and can be copied. • If no copies are available, retrieve the original or backup copy of the software from the storage facility. • If no backup copies are available, obtain replacement software from vendor. • Load software. • Verify the operation of the replacement software.	
5.	*Retrieve and load backup tapes* • Obtain PC backup tapes from off-site storage facilities. • Restore backup tapes to the PC assigned. • Verify the data loaded successfully. • Return backup tapes to the off-site storage facility.	**Vendor Name** **Telephone Number** **Contact Name**
6.	*Install new PCs and printers* • Backup all data on the PC. • Install all boards and test the new PCs. • Verify all software and data loaded correctly. • Provide accounting with a list of all new equipment, locations, and serial numbers.	
7.	Report status and actions taken to the Technology Recovery Team Leader who, in turn, will notify the EMT.	Technology Recovery Team

Damage Assessment Form

Refer to "Resource Item Matrix" to determine item requirements. Use this form to identify repair/replacement requirements.

Item	Location	Status (Recoverable/Lost)

Facilities Recovery Team

Team Contact Sheet

Team Functions:	Coordinates recovery operations of the Facilities following a disaster.
Alternate Site:	Recovery Center

Facilities Recovery Team Succession List

The first person on the list is the team/task force leader. If that person is not available, the second person becomes the team/task force leader, and so on.

First Name	Last Name	Home phone	Mobile phone	Beeper
JAMES	PANDA			
BRIAN	MALO			
BRUCE	MATHIS			

Facility Task Force

First Name	Last Name	Home phone	Mobile phone	Beeper
Accounting				
BRUCE	MATHIS			
RONALD	BROTHERS			
Facilities				
NANCY	ROME			
LIZZIE	LATTIMER			
Human Resources				
BRIAN	MALO			
ARRIE	WILLS			
GRACIE	LEENY			
KIMBERLY	HUREY			

Recover Facility

	Procedure	Default Vendor: **Vendor Name** **Telephone Number** **Contact Name** Tasks in this procedure should be assigned to the Facilities Task Force. Task force members may call on the services of other Facilities personnel who are not members of the recovery team.

1.	*Inspect structural integrity* If the advisability of reoccupying the structure is questionable: • Examine the facility to determine if it is safe for occupancy. • Photograph ALL damage for insurance purposes. If the structure is deemed safe and usable, continue with the procedure. If the facility can be re-occupied with repairs and clean up, continue with this procedure. If the structure can never be reoccupied, proceed to "Contact Insurance Representative" task and then to "move to temporary work space" task. If required, contact security vendor and arrange for building security services.	Record finding on the "Damage Assessment Form" at the end of the Facilities Recovery Team's Procedures. **Vendor Name** **Telephone Number** **Contact Name**
2.	*Inspect for non-structural damage* • Inspect facility and assess extent of non-structural damage, evaluate all equipment for salvage, repair or replacement. • Determine if power, ventilation, lighting, heating, and cooling are available or can be readily restored. • Determine requirements to repair windows, doors, and roof. • Determine requirement for water removal. • Determine requirement for mud and dirt removal. • Evaluate facility for reoccupation now, later (how long?), or never. • Relay findings of steps 1 and 2 to the EMT.	**Vendor Name** **Telephone Number** **Contact Name**
3.	*Clear access* If access to the facility is blocked: • Assess the amount and type of blockage. • Contact Facilities Management and arrange for removal service. • Determine vendor's time of arrival and estimated charges. • Monitor the progress of the work.	
4.	*Repair windows/doors* If windows or doors are damaged: • Determine the dimensions of the damaged windows/doors. • Contact Facilities Management and arrange for repair services. • Determine the estimated time of the vendor's arrival. • Determine the estimated cost of repair services. • If the repair time estimates exceed requirements, obtain boards, plywood, or plastic sheeting from the Facilities Department to temporarily seal off opening. • Monitor the progress of the work.	

5.	*Repair roof damage*	
	If the roof to the facility has been damaged:	
	• Assess the extent of the damage (type and size of damage). • Contact Facilities Management and arrange for repair services. • Determine vendor time of arrival, time for repair, and estimated cost of repairs. • Monitor the progress of the work.	
6.	*Remove water*	
	If the facility has excessive water that needs to be removed and water is close to or touching electrical sources, call the fire department for water removal. Otherwise:	
	• Call listed vendor for water removal services. • Call Facilities Management for repair of pipes/bathroom facilities. • Determine time of vendor arrival and estimated cost of repair. • Monitor the progress of the work. • Use fans to dry out area after the work is completed.	
7.	*Repair electrical malfunction*	**Vendor Name** **Telephone Number** **Contact Name**
	If, after examination, damage to the structure's internal electrical system is suspected:	
	• Contact Facilities Management and arrange for testing and repair of the structure's electrical system. • Determine the estimated time of the vendor's arrival. • Determine the estimated cost of the service. • Monitor the progress of the repairs.	
8.	*Obtain emergency power*	**Vendor Name** **Telephone Number** **Contact Name**
	If electrical power is not available:	
	• Confirm outage with the power company and expected duration. • Obtain sufficient fuel to run the generator for the anticipated duration of the outage. Notify fuel vendor for additional requirements.	
9.	*Remove mud/dirt from facility*	
	If the facility has dirt and mud inside:	
	• Contact Facilities Management or other vendor and arrange for a clean up. • Determine the estimated time of the vendor's arrival. • Determine the estimated cost of the service. • Monitor the progress of the clean up.	

10.	*Contact insurance representative* If it is determined that damage has been done to the facility: ● As phone service becomes available, contact corporate insurance department and describe the extent of the damage that has been observed. ● Determine what the insurance provider requires prior to taking any action. ● Contact Insurance Adjuster. ● Use vendor estimates to document damage. ● Update insurance department on actions taken and expenses incurred.	**Vendor Name** **Telephone Number** **Contact Name**
11.	*Move to temporary location* If primary facility will be uninhabitable for 10 working days or more, move staff to alternate work space: ● Notify commercial real estate broker of need for temporary work space. ● Notify staff of temporary site, space allocations, and planned length of stay. ● Notify customers and vendors of new location and phone number. Maintain communications with customer base until normal operations resume. ● Determine estimated time of reoccupying permanent facility. ● Arrange for transport services for critical and salvageable resource items (determine if staff will use their own vehicles to assist in this effort). ● Transport as many resource items that can be salvaged to the temporary site. Notify customers and vendors of the new location. ● Enter new address and telephone number on the Web site.	**Vendor Name** **Telephone Number** **Contact Name** Customer Service and Sales Task Forces
12.	*Ready permanent workspace* If the existing facility needs major repairs or if an entirely new facility needs to be found: ● Assess equipment, furniture, electrical, and phone needs for permanent facility. ● Retain contractor and architect for construction services. ● Work with vendors to develop a layout of the facility that includes the placement of equipment, cables and lease lines, furniture, electrical outlets and telephones. ● Authorize construction. ● Distribute a copy of the layout to those who will need to instruct service providers and vendors regarding delivery. ● Monitor progress of construction activities.	**Vendor Name** **Telephone Number** **Contact Name**

13.	*Reoccupy facility* • Receive notification that the facility is ready to be occupied. • Arrange with staff or with local vendor to provide for moving from temporary space into the permanent facility. • Move from temporary facility to permanent facility. • Switch telephone numbers back to the permanent facility. • Inform members, customers and vendors of the move to the permanent facility (list on Web site) • Enter voice message on 800 number	Customer Service Task Force
14.	Report status and actions taken to the Facilities Recovery Team Leader who, in turn, will notify the EMT.	

Recover Off-site Records and Documentation

Procedure	Tasks in this procedure should be assigned to a Facilities Team member. This team member may call on the services of other Facilities personnel who are not members of the recovery team.
1. *Damage assessment of records* • Inventory vital records and documents using "Storage Location Detail Report". • Identify those records that are critical, are backed up, and need to be replaced. • Retrieve available records from off-site records storage.	**Vendor Name** **Telephone Number** **Contact Name** Record findings on the "Damage Assessment Form" at the end of the Facilities Recovery Team's Procedures.
2. *Document restoration* • Identify critical documents that are water or fire damaged but might be restored. • Contact vendor for assistance in restoring documents. • Identify and document destroyed vital documents. • Submit record of damages to insurance unit.	**Vendor Name** **Telephone Number** **Contact Name**
3. Report status and actions taken to the Facilities Recovery Team Leader who, in turn, will notify the EMT.	

Replace Staff

	Procedure	Tasks in this procedure should be assigned to the Human Resources Task Force. Task force members may call on the services of other personnel who are not members of the recovery team.
1.	*Staff assessment* • Attempt to establish contact with each staff member using the "Detail Staff List". • If telephone functions are available, use telephone to establish contact. • If telephone communication is not available, go to staff members' home residences to establish contact. • Communicate disaster situation, actions taken, and possible need for their help in replacing missing team members. • Determine missing or unavailable staff members. • Relay findings to the EMT.	
2.	*Replenish teams* • Verify that teams have sufficient staff to cover all tasks assigned in the action plan. • If teams are not fully staffed, use the "Detail Staff List" to identify staff members who could fill open team positions. • Contact staff members identified in the previous step and request their assistance. • When the staff member joins the team, give a brief description of the disaster recovery process and what role you expect this staff member to play. • Assign the staff member his or her duties.	
3.	*Temporary staff* If there is a need for additional staff and all staff resources have been depleted, temporary help may be required: • Contact personnel department or vendor directly to acquire the quantity and quality of employees needed. • Interview and acquire the quantity of employees needed by required skill level. • Arrange for the new employees' transportation and lodging if necessary.	**Vendor Name** **Telephone Number** **Contact Name**

4.	*Payroll continuity* • Track hourly staff's time on timesheets and send to personnel/payroll on a timely basis. • If payroll services are not available internally, send timesheets directly to payroll vendor for processing.	Accounting Task Force **Vendor Name** **Telephone Number** **Contact Name**
5.	Report status and actions taken to the Facilities Recovery Team Leader who, in turn, will notify the EMT.	

Recover Office Furniture

	Procedure	Tasks in this procedure should be assigned to a Facilities Team member. This team member may call on the services of other Facilities personnel who are not members of the recovery team
1.	*Damage assessment* • Make an assessment of the damage and replacement needs using the "Resource Item Matrix" report. • Compile a report of missing or damaged items that need to be replaced or repaired. • Salvage and safeguard as many resources items as possible. • Relay findings to the EMT.	Record finding on the "Damage Assessment Form" at the end of the Facilities Recovery Team's Procedures.
2.	*Recover office furniture* • Locate the "Resource Item Matrix" report. • Determine types and quantities of office furniture required. • Poll other facilities to determine what office furniture can be borrowed on a short-term basis. • For required furniture that cannot be obtained internally, contact vendors and acquire the appropriate quantities of office furniture. • If vendor delivery is available, arrange for time of delivery.	**Vendor Name** **Telephone Number** **Contact Name**
3.	*Plan for furniture replacement* • Design a layout of the placement of the office furniture that will be delivered. • If a move is required, coordinate the layout design with the senior manager of the temporary facility. • Distribute a copy of the layout to those who will be instructing vendors regarding deliveries of office furniture.	

4.	*Arrange for transportation* If office furniture vendor is unable to provide transportation: ● Poll staff to determine if transportation services are available internally. ● Contact moving vendor and make arrangements to move items to new location. ● Obtain time of move, cost and method of payment required. ● Alert staff member at move destination of impending delivery. ● Monitor delivery of goods. ● Provide Accounting with a list of all new furniture and its location.	**Vendor Name** **Telephone Number** **Contact Name**
5.	Report status and actions taken to the Facilities Recovery Team Leader who, in turn, will notify the EMT.	

Recover Office Equipment

	Procedure	Tasks in this procedure should be assigned to a Facilities Task Force. Task force members may call on the services of other personnel who are not members of the recovery team
1.	*Damage assessment* ● Make an assessment of the damage and replacement needs using the "Resource Item Matrix" report. ● Compile a report of missing or damaged items that need to be replaced or repaired. ● Salvage and safeguard as many resources items as possible. ● Relay findings to the EMT.	Record finding on the "Damage Assessment Form" at the end of the Facilities Recovery Team's Procedures.
2.	*Damage mitigation* If equipment is or has been exposed to moisture, remove it from electrical power sources (main power, electrical generator, UPS). ● If the environment is contaminated, remove equipment and electromagnetic media to a controlled environment free from smoke, soot, water, and high humidity. ● Prior to removal, label equipment to identify its home location and any other equipment to which it was connected.	**Vendor Name** **Telephone Number** **Contact Name**

	• Wipe off all moisture from outside of electromagnetic media (diskettes, tapes, CDs). • Obtain written consent of manufacturer and vendors for the disaster procedures being taken on equipment under warranty or maintenance contract. • Do not allow vendors/staff to test, evaluate or diagnose damage prior to restoration. • Let the vendor de-install, re-install, then re-certify equipment. • Move damaged equipment into storage until an adjuster can look at it. • Prior to re-installation, ensure that surge protectors have remained functional.	
3.	*Recover office equipment* • Locate the "Resource Item Matrix" report. • Determine the types and quantities of office equipment required. • Poll other locations to determine what equipment can be borrowed on a short-term basis. • For required equipment that cannot be obtained internally, contact vendors and order the appropriate quantities of equipment. • Indicate the address and location for delivery. • Provide Accounting with a list of all new equipment, locations, and serial numbers.	**Vendor Name** **Telephone Number** **Contact Name**
4.	*Plan equipment placement* • Design a layout of the placement of the equipment that will be delivered. • If a move to a temporary facility is required, coordinate layout design with senior manager of temporary facility. • Distribute a copy of the layout to those who will be instructing vendors regarding deliveries of equipment.	
5.	Report status and actions taken to the Facilities Recovery Team Leader who, in turn, will notify the EMT.	

Recover Stationery and Supplies

	Procedure	Tasks in this procedure should be assigned to a Facilities team member. This team member may call on the services of other Facilities personnel who are not members of the recovery team.

1.	*Damage assessment* • Make an assessment of the damage and replacement needs using the "Resource Item Matrix" report. • Compile a report of missing or damaged items that need to be replaced or repaired. • Salvage and safeguard as many resources items as possible.	Record finding on the "Damage Assessment Form" at the end of the Facilities Recovery Team's Procedures.
2.	*Recover office supplies* • Compile a list of the quantities of the supplies needed by examining Supplies report. • Contact the appropriate vendors and order supplies. • Monitor the delivery of the supplies.	See "Supplies"
3.	Report status and actions taken to the Facilities Recovery Team Leader who, in turn, will notify the EMT.	

Recover Ground Communications Services

	Procedure	Tasks in this procedure should be assigned to a Facilities team member. This team member may call on the services of other Facilities personnel who are not members of the recovery team
1.	*Recover postal services* If an alternative facility is being used by staff members to conduct business: • Notify post office and private postal vendors (FedEx, Airborne, etc., see Detail Vendor Listing) of the new location. • Fill out change of address cards in order to notify customers. • If postal service is unable to deliver mail, set up a schedule of periodic "Hold Mail" pickups. • Notify mailroom personnel of the location of all staff. • When permanent facility is ready, notify post office and private postal vendors of the new location. • Use change of address cards to notify customers of change back to original facility.	
2.	Report status and actions taken to the Facilities Recovery Team Leader who, in turn, will notify the EMT.	

Provide Human Comforts and Support

	Procedure	Tasks in this procedure should be assigned to the Human Resources Task Force. Task force members may call on the services of other Facilities personnel who are not members of the recovery team
1.	*Support assessment* Determine and provide needed supplies and services for staff support during recovery operation (food, water, and bedding). Determine cash requirements for a 20-day period and determine if local financial institutions are capable of providing requirements.	Accounting Task Force
2.	*Arrange travel and hotel* • Determine the number of people traveling and/or needing hotel accommodation. • Make travel and hotel arrangements. • Receive verification of staff arrival and update contact lists.	
3.	*Arrange showers and rest* If conditions warrant: • Arrange with local hotel facilities for room(s) to clean up and rest for restoration purposes. • Arrange transportation to and from the facility.	
4.	*Provide food and drink* If the disaster condition is such that staff members are unable to obtain food and liquids as they normally would: • Determine the number of people for whom food and drink must be provided. • Identify vendors who are in close proximity that can accommodate food and drink requirements. • Purchase food and drink supplies. • Keep food service areas sanitary. • Provide clean drinking water.	
5.	*Acquire cash* Acquire cash for 20-day period if deemed necessary.	Accounting Task Force
6.	Report status and actions taken to the Facilities Recovery Team Leader who, in turn, will notify the EMT.	

Damage Assessment Form

Refer to "Resource Item Matrix" to determine item requirements. Use this form to identify repair/replacement requirements.

Item	Location	Status (Recoverable/Lost)

Order Processing Team

	Team Contact Sheet
Team Functions:	**Coordinates the maintenance of Customer and Member relations. Reduces the Exchange's liability from Order book non-executions.**
Alternate Site:	**Recovery Center**

Order Processing Team Succession List

The first person on the list is the team/task force leader. If that person is not available, the second person becomes the team/task force leader, and so on.

First Name	Last Name	Home Phone	Mobile Phone	Beeper
ANDREW	KOL			
SUSAN	MILLS			
ADAM	SCHNEIR			

Public Relations Task Force

First Name	Last Name	Home Phone	Mobile Phone	Beeper
LISA	CERVE			
RIVA	HEM			

Customer Service Task Force

First Name	Last Name	Home Phone	Mobile Phone	Beeper
SUSAN	MILLS			
ELAINE	STRO			
ERIC	WHILE			
KEVIN	TYS			
JOEL	ZAW			
BRIAN	GIO			
BRETT	MILLS			
JOHN	CASTER			
RALPH	BARR			

Maintain Media Relations

	Procedure	Public Relations Task Force
1.	*Receive authorization from EMT Manager* • Receive notification that a disaster has been declared. • Receive authorization from EMT Manager to contact the news media. • Contact all division managers and inform them that none of their staff are to discuss the emergency situation with the news media.	
2.	*Identify facts of situation* • Retrieve Media Relations Fact Sheet • Contact Business Continuity Coordinator to complete Fact Sheet.	See "Media Relations Fact Sheet"
3.	*Prepare statement* • Use Media Relations template to complete media statement. • Review statement with EMT Manager. • Receive EMT manager approval.	During this stage, you may want to contact PR consulting firm: **Vendor Name** **Telephone Number** **Contact Name**
4.	*Contact media representatives* • Identify media representatives using Media Contact List. • Determine media representatives to contact.	See "Media Contact List"
5.	*Release message to media* • Release prepared statement to print media representatives. • If requested, give structured interviews to radio and TV news media.	Release via *PR Newswire* to appropriate wires (PR Newswire rep. can help determine which wires are best, may want to select nationwide distribution) Also, may want to "blast fax" to media list. Contact: **Vendor Name** **Telephone Number** **Contact Name** Request the "long" media list. Final steps: phone media to make sure release was received and post release to the Web site if possible.
6.	*End of procedure* Report status and actions taken to the Order Processing Team Leader who, in turn, will notify the EMT.	

Maintain Customer/Member Relations

	Procedure	Sales Task Force
1.	*Receive authorization from EMT manager* • Receive notification that a disaster has been declared. • Receive authorization from EMT Manager to contact the Customers and Exchange Members.	
2.	*Identify facts of situation* • Retrieve Media Relations Fact Sheet • Contact Business Continuity Coordinator to complete Fact Sheet.	
3.	*Prepare statements* • Use Customer Relations template to complete statement. • Review statement with EMT Manager. • Receive EMT manager approval.	
4.	*Contact customer representatives* • Select customers to be contacted. • Review statement with customer. • Advise customer of continuing communications. • Contact customer again when promised.	See "Order Sending Firms E-mail/Phone Number Listing"
5.	*End of procedure* • When emergency condition terminates and operations return to normal, contact customers and members and inform them of the situation. • Report status and actions taken to the Order Processing Team Leader who, in turn, will notify the EMT.	

Damage Assessment Form

Refer to "Resource Item Matrix" to determine item requirements. Use this form to identify repair/replacement requirements.

Item	Location	Status (Recoverable/Lost)

At the end of each team's set of procedures there is a damage assessment form. This form should be used to gather damage information so that it can be reported to the EMT. This also becomes a valuable document for legal and insurance purposes.

Throughout the Action Plan, there are references to a number of lists and tables. Below are abbreviated examples of standard tables that should be part of any BCP:

RESOURCE ITEM MATRIX

This report lists the minimum resources required to reestablish a function. For each item listed, look in the right-hand column to find the total amount of an item required. This should be used when making an order with a vendor.

The columns to the left of the Total column are the departmental requirements. These will be used for the distribution of the item once the vendor has delivered them.

The BIA DURATION ASSESSMENT line represents the amount of time the organization can continue without the service before severe financial consequences occur. This, then, is the recovery time objective for each service/department.

	Applications Development	Cust. Svs / Systems Support	Data / Telecomm / IS Facilities	Facilities	Facilities Security	Financial Services	Human Resources	IS Operations	IS Support Services	Legal & Office of the Secretary	Listing	National Sales	Marketing	Market Regulation	Market Regulation / Surveillance	Trading Floor Operations	TOTAL
BIA DURATION ASSESSMENT	2-5	2-5	0-2	>10	>10	>10	>10	0-2	0-2	>10	2-5	>10	0-2	5-10	5-10	0-2	
ITEMS																	
DATA COMMUNICATIONS	(See Data Communications Appendix)																
FACILITIES																	
Meeting Rooms	200		100			100		100						100		100	700
Office Space (100 sq. ft./person)	6900	2400	800	500	200	1500	400	1500	2500	300	300	600	600	1000	800	24500	44800
Storage Space		300	800		100	200	100			100	100	100	100	100	100	100	2200
Mail Room			1000														1000
Forms Storage			5000														5000
Lab	600																600
Control Center								500									500
	1	2	3	4	5	6	7	8	9	10	11	12	13	14	15	16	
Computer Center								4000									4000
MICROCOMPUTERS																	
Security Access Systems				2													2
UPS				1													1

	1	2	3	4	5	6	7	8	9	10	11	12	13	14	15	16	Total
OFFICE EQUIPMENT																	
Calculator		24	8		1	15	2	1			1		2	5		6	65
Copier	1	1	1			1	1	1	1		1		1	1	1	2	13
Fax	1	1	1	1	1	1	1		1		1		1	2	1	5	18
Postage Meter/Scales				1													1
Shredder		1					1										2
Typewriter		1			1		1						1		1		5
Photo ID System					1												1
Laminator					1												1
OFFICE FURNITURE																	
Chairs	95	24	15	5	2	21	10	31	20	3	3	6	7	16	16	51	325
Computer Racks		40						30									70
Desks	69	24	9	5	2	15	4	10	25	3	3	6	5	10	8	25	223
File Cabinets	69		3		1	30	1	1				4	1	10		20	140
Tables	7		10		1	10	2	8	6				1	1		10	56
Shelf Units		3	4					1									8
Mail Sorting Bin (Set)				1													1
Beds									8								8
OFF-SITE STORAGE																	
Cust. Service Paper Trail		1															1
PBX Backup Tapes (Inacom)			1														1
PBX Backup Tapes (Siemans)			1														1
Trading Floor Forms				1													1
Letter Head Stationery (Box)			1														1
Financial Records							1										1
Legal Files										1							1
Old Files (boxes)											300	2					302
Files													1	1		1	3
HR Records							1										1
SOFTWARE	(See Software Appendix)																
STAFF																	
IS Managers	6																6
Data Base Administrators	3																3
Programmer Analysts	30																30
Systems Analysts	30	1															31
Attorney		2								3							5
Exchange Customer Service		5															5
CSR I		16															16
CSR II		1															1
CSR Supervisor		3															3
Administrative Assistant		1											1				2
CSR Manager		1															1
DataComm Engineer			3														3
Telecomm Engineer			2														2
Billing Coordinator			1														1
MAC Coordinator			1														1
Network Documentor			1														1
Mail Room Clerk				3													3
Facilities Coordinator				1													1
Facilities Manager				1													1
Site Security Supervisor					1												1
Security Administrator					1												1
CFO						1											1
Accounting Clerks						7											7
Clerical Staff						3					1					27	31
Accounting Supervisor						2											2
Accounting Manager						2					1						3

																	Total
Technical Recruiter							2										2
Non-technical Recruiter							2										2
Computer Operator								8									8
Operations Analysts								4									4
Operations Manager								3									3
Network Specialists									3								3
NT Server Specialists									3								3
Data Comm. Specialist									3								3
Telecomm Specialist									3								3
VMS Specialist									3								3
UNIX Specialist									1								1
Project Manager									4								4
PC Support Analyst									8								8
Managerial Finance										1							1
Sales Manager												1					1
Sales Rep.												4					4
Sales Analyst												1					1
Public Relations Manager													1				1
Marketing Coordinator													2				2
Receptionist													1				1
Web Person													1				1
Marketing Director													1				1
Risk Analyst														1			1
Financial (Compliance) Examiner														4			4
Manager														4		2	6
Senior Manager														1			1
Senior Level Exchange Officer															1		1
Data Entry Clerks																12	12
Supervisors																4	4
TOTAL	**69**	**30**	**8**	**5**	**2**	**15**	**4**	**15**	**28**	**3**	**3**	**7**	**6**	**10**	**1**	**45**	**251**
SUPPLIES	(See Supplies Appendix)																
Status Pads (Box of 5000)		1															1
2 Ply Paper (Boxes)		30															30
Cat 5 Wiring (rolls)									200								200
Security Badges				300													300
Federal Securities Law Reporter										1							1
Forms (See Forms Appendix)																	
TELECOMMUNICATIONS																	
Mobile Phones	15	1	6	2		1	1	5	25			4	2	1	2		65
Pagers	30	4	8	2				15	25				2		8	7	101
PBX			2														2
Telephone Console													1				1
Telephones	69	24	12		2	15	5	30	6	3	3	7	5	10	8	33	232
Headsets		24		5													29
Nextel Direct Connect				2													2
Walkie Talkies				4													4

DETAIL STAFF LIST

Last Name	First Name	Title	Organization Chart	Address	City	St	Zip	Phone
Ahmad	Hasan	SR ENGINEER	Product Creation	422 Kings Brook Dr				
Aiken	Christopher	PROGRAMMER	Product Creation	113 Valley View Road				
Ambe	Prashant	SR. MGR TECHNICAL	Product Creation	469 Diablo Drive				
Andree	Joy	ADMIN ASSISTANT	Product Creation	23 First Street				
Bacik	Kathy	SUPPORT ANALYST	Accounting	16 Green Glen Drive				
Barbour	Barbara	ADMIN ASSOCIATE	Product Creation	348 Houston Street				
Bayani	Victor	SR. MGR TECHNICAL	Product Creation	P.O. Box 4567				
Beach	Marie	MANAGER— ADMIN	Product Licensing & Auth	1000 Ajay Drive				
Beck Fortna	Deborah	SR. SUPERVISOR	Accounting	178 Markwood Drive				
Bemis	Paul	VICE PRESIDENT	Marketing	185 Spring Meadow Drive				

Staff Detail by Department

Accounting

Bacik	Kathy	SUPPORT ANALYST	16 Green Glen Drive
Beck Fortna	Deborah	SR. SUPERVISOR	178 Markwood Drive
Bossong Jr.	Charles	SR. ACCOUNTANT	5323 Sutton Place Ext.
Day	Michael	ACCOUNTANT	P. O. Box 84
Detwiler	Marshall	SR. MANAGER	8147 Nixon Road
Krawczewicz	Vivian	ACCOUNTANT	3702 Poplar Ave
Richardson	Marsha	ACCOUNTANT	136 McClellan Drive
Smith	Joanne	ADMIN CLERK	510-D Main Street
Warburton	John	ACCOUNTANT	674 Aljo Drive

Corporate Quality

Bryan	William	SR. MGR TECHNICAL	168 Lakeview Drive
Podlaszewski	Kenneth	ENGINEERS	220 McClane Farm Rd
Podolek	Bonny	ADMIN ASSISTANT	109 McElree Road

Customer Service

Bryan	Joann	SR ENGINEER	168 Lakeview Drive
Chang	Susan	ENGINEERS	2917 Big Meadow Rd
Chilensky	Paul	DEPT HEAD	342 Birch Street

DETAIL VENDOR LISTING

Arch Paging
180 Fort Couch Road, Suite 150 Pittsburgh, Pa 15241

Work Phone	Fax Number	Mobile Phone	First Name	Last Name
(412) 854–2300	(412) 854–2498	(412) 590–9977	Brian	Fuller

Title
Sales Representative

Notes
IT Text pagers; systems programmed to automatically send SMC personnel backup statuses; also used to send urgent help desk request messages to IT staff

Asset Recovery Technologies, Inc.
2625 American Lane
Elk Grove Village IL 60007-

Work Phone	Fax Number	Mobile Phone	First Name	Last Name
(800) 805–0644			Lawrie	Ackerman

Title
President
Notes
AKA The Price-Hollingsworth Company, Inc. Recovery of Electrical/Electronic and Mechanical Equipment. Mitigates and recovers disasters arising from fire and flood.

AT&T

Work Phone	Fax Number	Mobile Phone	First Name	Last Name
(412) 316–9909			Dan	Hixenbaugh

Title

Notes
Local telephone service. 479 DID Numbers.

The Vendor List is one of the most important schedules in a disaster recovery. This list should include direct telephone numbers for the vendor representative that can help your organization (you do not want to have to go through a series of button pushing and elevator music trying to get to the right person). It should also contain critical information in the "Notes" section such as account numbers and descriptions of services/products provided. A well-documented "Notes" section makes the Vendor List powerful.

INSURANCE VENDOR LISTING

Company Name
Adjusters International
Address
126 Business Park Drive, Utica NY 13503

Work Phone	First Name	Last Name	Title	Mobile Phone
(800) 382–2468	John	Martini	Director of Sales	

Fax Number

Notes
Aligned with Globe Midwest in a national confederation of insurance adjusters.

PLAN LOCATION

First Name	Last Name	Title	Plan Location
Kathy	Bacik	SUPPORT ANALYST	Home
Marie	Beach	MANAGER—ADMIN	Office
Vedran	Bender	COMPUTER ADMIN	Home

There are numerous other lists that can be included such as Customer lists, Computer Software and Hardware inventories, Communication Schematics, etc. During the BIA interview process, ask each interviewee to imagine standing outside their burning building and thinking what valuable piece of information is still located inside that they didn't have time to rescue (probably located in their right top drawer of their desk). These are many times the "cheat sheets" that managers use to manage their departments. These are the types of information that rightfully belong as part of the plan.

DOCUMENTATION RULES

There are several documentation rules that will make the plan much more effective. The first rule is one plan, one building. Much of the plan revolves around reconstructing a facility and replenishing it with production contents. If more than one facility is involved, then the reader of the plan will find it difficult to identify quantities and specifications of replacement resource items. It is possible to have multiple plans for a single building, but those plans must be linked so that the identification and ordering of resource items is centralized.

The second rule is to begin each Task statement with an action verb. Tasks are supposed to be predetermined actions that are to be taken by the teams. Along this line of thought, there should not be requirements to form a committee to decide on a course of action. These decisions should be made ahead of time and incorporated into the plan.

Third, refer to functions, not a specific person in procedures/tasks. Instead of "Contact Joe Smith for assistance with . . ." write "Contact the Network Administrator for assistance with . . .". The second statement will then be valid in the event that Joe Smith leaves the company.

Fourth, call critical vendors ahead of time. If the plan assumes that 40 servers can be obtained from a certain computer equipment supplier, a call should be made to that supplier to verify that 40 servers could be delivered in the required timeframe. The supplier should also be questioned about who would get priority in the event of an area-wide disaster.

Fifth, avoid re-keying whenever possible. Ask business unit managers if the data you seek (staff lists, vendor lists, customer lists, etc.) already exist in electronic form. If they exist in Access or Excel, then it should be quite easy to load the database and transform it into reports that can be used in the plan. Otherwise, plan on a good deal of time being spent on data input.

Sixth, anticipate delays; get large item requests in early. The four items that tend to be the most difficult to get in a timely manner are the Staff List, the Vendor List, the Customer List, and Information Systems Information (equipment and software inventories, communications inventories and schematics, and equipment schematics). Once this information is obtained, it is important to interview each of the respondents to verify the currency and accuracy of the information.

Finally, utilize the "Straw-man" technique wherever possible. The straw-man technique is presenting a prepared document to the client and allowing the client to make modifications and changes to the document. The technique can be used with strategies, team lists, and action plans. This method is very efficient with the client's time and will get the client to focus quickly on his/her thoughts and buy-in to the plan document. When creating the action plan, have the team members that will be performing the recovery procedures gather around your PC's CRT and go through each task line by line. Let the team decide how the tasks are worded and structured. At the end, this will be an action plan that the team has created and can execute.

6 Testing and Maintenance

The plan has now been completed and approved by the senior management of the organization. Two more requirements remain. The plan must be tested and it must be maintained.

TESTING

Testing determines if documented recovery strategies and associated recovery procedures are viable to recover critical business functions within their stated recovery time objectives. Testing validates planning assumptions and it identifies the strengths and weaknesses in the plan.

It is recommended that testing does not exceed established frequency limits. For a plan to be effective, all components of the BCP should be tested at least once a year. If there is a major change in the operations of the organization, the plan should be revised and tested not more than three months after the change becomes operational.

For a test to truly demonstrate the effectiveness of the plan, all units should be tested together. Units that are not used to working together may have to coordinate their efforts during an emergency situation. It is better to understand and correct coordination problems before an actual emergency is encountered.

You must have a plan for a test. Within the plan there should be a test scope and objectives, a test scenario, a recovery sequence, and a test schedule. The following is an example of a test plan:

I. TEST CLASSIFICATION

A. *PRODUCTION PROCESSING ENVIRONMENT AND BACKUP SITE*

This exercise is intended to test The Company (TC)'s ability to recover the fundamental Operating System/Applications and re-establish the production environment for ABC Data Center in the backup center in Compterville, Nevada.

The ABC Data Center is comprised of:

— 10 Production Stratus 310, 320, 330 type CPUs;
— A Data General MV60000 CPU for back-end processing;
— Dedicated telecommunications links for Frame Relay, Deluxer and dial-in access.

To support this environment for Disaster Recovery, TC has developed its own internal hardware infrastructure in Compterville, Nevada. This infrastructure consists of:

— 10 Stratus CPUs;
— A Data General MV60000 that performs back-end processing;
— Dedicated telecommunications links for Deluxer and dial-in access.

This backup hardware in Compterville, Nevada is dedicated to the recovery of these platforms in the event of a disaster in the ABC Data Center. This Disaster Recovery hardware is located in TC's Compterville Data Center. Built into this data center is full connectivity to all ABC customers.

The recovery is structured so that both platforms can be recovered within 4 hours in Compterville. Both platforms (Stratus and Data General) are powered up with an operating system running, system/application software, and applications data recovered. The Merchant master files and application software on these platforms are very stagnant and, as a result, TC has a process in place which applies updates to these files on a weekly basis. TC ships backups of this data and software from ABC to Compterville overnight on a weekly basis and by transmitting files directly to Compterville. These tapes are then applied to the Stratus and Data General systems that night.

The testing itself will be done from the Compterville, Nevada Data Center. TC's Disaster Recovery Team will facilitate the test. The consultant will also be monitoring the test to ensure that procedures are being followed and any exceptions being noted. There will be sufficient System Administrators and Operations staff on-site to conduct the test. Applications support will be provided by the production applications support staff in the respective locations. Connectivity for this support will be done with its current LAN infrastructure.

B. *TEST DATES AND TIMES*

The test dates for the exercise are April 22, 1999 at 04:00 EDT through April 22, 1999 at 06:00 EDT. The assumed disaster date will be April 22, 1999. The test will be 27 contiguous hours in duration. The date set on the CPU at the test will be April 22, 1999, and the time will be "wall clock time CDT". Due to the duration of the test,

TC will designate specific staff who will occupy the multiple shifts required to complete it. Attached to this document is a copy of the shift schedule. A designated TC Test Team will conduct the test.

C. *TEST LOCATION AND HARDWARE*

Again, the Disaster Recovery hardware in Compterville, Nevada mimics the production environment in ABC, Washington. This equipment was purchased/leased for the purpose of backup for the ABC Data Center. The environment consists of the following hardware:

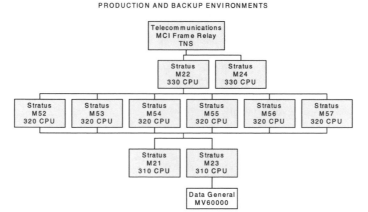

PRODUCTION AND BACKUP ENVIRONMENTS

To gain an understanding of how the data were moved from ABC to Compterville, one must understand the production environment. The Production Stratus CPUs in ABC are set up in a mirrored disk environment as depicted in the following outline:

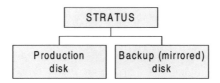

Each system has a production and a backup (or mirrored) disk. The DR systems in Compterville were developed by first performing a logical then physical split of the production/backup disk in ABC. This was done by performing the following:

- The disks purchased for Compterville were shipped into ABC.
- The backup mirrored disks in ABC were removed and production ran from the single set of disks.

- The new disks from Compterville were then inserted into the ABC backup disk slots.
- The production data disks were then copied to the mirrored disk. This took any-where from 5 minutes to 1.5 hours per disk.
- The original backup mirrored disks which were pulled from the production Stratus CPU, were shipped to Compterville.
- Once the disks arrived in Compterville, they were inserted into the respective Stratus CPUs as the primary disk.
- In Compterville, a process was then initiated to copy the production disk to the backup mirrored disk.
- A process of clearing both the CIF database on the Stratus and the GDB data-base on the Data General is performed. Once this is completed, both the produc-tion and mirrored disk are synchronized. The baseline systems are now developed and the systems are available for DR testing or recovery.

Weekly backups are taken on the Data General and Stratus processors in ABC and shipped to Compterville where they are applied to the DR systems. Weekly backups are sufficient as the information located on the databases is relatively stagnant. This synchronization takes approximately 6 hours.

D. *TEST LOCATION PHONE NUMBERS:*

Compterville Data Center for Stratus: 999–555-4262
Compterville Data Center for Data General: 999–555-7325.

E. *ASSUMPTIONS*

1. That no live transactions will be run through the Disaster Recovery test. Only test transactions will be used for the test
2. The system is functional and the plan is written as if it were a real disaster with the exception of providing telecommunications connectivity to all banks and clients.
3. Telecommunications connectivity via TNS will occur to enter the test transactions as if a merchant were entering the transactions. All eight production cut-offs will be run at their normal timeframes. All reports and microfiche will be produced but not sent out to clients or users. A Help Desk representative will be performing the online portion of the test. Since the Stratus and Data General CPUs don't support an automated job scheduler, all batch processes will be run manually as they do today in production. Testing on the Stratus CPUs will be conducted solely from the mirrored disk. This will preserve the baseline system on the production disk in case of a true disaster in ABC. This does not affect the outcome of the test. Those data were copied disk-to-disk as part of the building of the CPUs in Compterville. The host would then be kept up to date with merchant data via weekly updates copied to tape from ABC.

II. TEST OBJECTIVES

A number of "Test Objectives" have been defined for this exercise. In addition to these objectives, this exercise is also intended to test the completeness and accuracy of the Disaster Recovery Procedures (either existing or subsequently developed) for this testing effort.

These procedures are essential for TC ABC Data Center's recovery. Consequently it is imperative that these procedures or guidelines reflect the sequential steps, tasks, job names, etc. needed to restore and run a production environment as described.

As a result of the above, this exercise addresses the issue of TC's recoverability at a redundant site. Any flaws or omissions occurring in this must be noted for correction to prepare for a disaster.

Again, the Test Objectives have been identified and will be met by following the documented test script. To monitor the progress of the test, MS Project will be utilized to monitor recovery timeframes and production runs. A copy of the timeline is attached to this document. The high-level objectives are as follows:

Hardware Infrastructure	Verify hardware: (10) Stratus processors consisting of Models 310, 320, 330 and (1) Data General Model MV60000 The baseline system for both the Stratus and Data General have been from March 20 to March 31, 1999. This was completed in ABC by selecting a point in time to both physically and logically separating the mirrored disk. At a selected point in time, the mirrors were broken and the backup disk was removed and shipped to Compterville. This disk was installed, the system booted and the databases were synchronized to the most current set of backups.
Operating Systems	Validate the STRATUS and Data General operating system software. Ensure that the STRATUS and Data General software that is resident on the mirrored disk in Compterville is complete and will function as required.
System Clean Up	***At the conclusion of the test TC will re-mirror the baseline disk to the Disaster Recovery testing disk.***
Databases	Validate the recoverability of the following: CIF (Stratus) GDB(Data General) Ensure the weekly backup tape from ABC has been applied.
Applications	Validate the recoverability of the following: CCSS RMS

Online/Batch	Data General online testing will be completed by a Help Desk representative who will process the Merchant updates. STRATUS batch cycles **Interchange, Janitor** and other critical batches as dictated by the timeline will be tested. Data General batch cycle will also be tested.
Network	Confirm connectivity. A TNS connection will be established to input the "test" transaction into the Authorization Process.

III. TEST EXIT/POST TEST AUDIT

The Disaster Recovery Coordinator (DRC) will be documenting the test as it actually occurs. Also on site will be an auditing consultant from Internal Audit and external consultants. The external consultant was hired by TC to have a third party monitor the test to ensure that procedures were being followed and to document issues that occurred during the test. Any issues from the test will be resolved as if there was an actual disaster.

After the test, the DRC will be issuing a post mortem of what actually occurred during the test. To accomplish this, the DRC will draft a copy of the post mortem that contains:

- Management summary
- Graphs showing what the goals and objectives estimated benchmarks were and how long they actually took
- Test issues with the associated Infoman records
- Detail of the test in the form of test notes
- Timeline from MS Project showing the detail of the estimated completion
- Time of tasks vs. actual completion time of tasks.

The DRC will then conduct a meeting to ensure that everyone has consensus of what actually occurred during the test. Then the final document will be distributed to senior management within TC.

In order to evaluate the test, there must be predefined criteria. A typical method used is to produce a set of reports during a live production period and then to try to produce exact copies of those reports using backed-up equipment, operating systems, software, and data. The test could then be evaluated upon the accuracy of the reports that were run with backed-up resources. The time required to produce the second set of data should be compared with the RTO as a further measure of the test's success.

Once the test is completed there should be follow-up activities to ensure identified action items are quickly resolved.

Testing can be done in parts (component testing) or all at once (full business testing). Component tests are actual physical exercises designed to assess the readiness and effectiveness of discrete plan elements and recovery activities. The isolation of key recovery activities allows team members to focus their efforts while limiting testing expense and resources. This methodology is effective for identifying and resolving issues that may adversely affect the successful completion of a full operations test.

The full business test requires extensive planning and preparation and should not be performed until most, if not all of the plan components have been tested. This test requires the simulated recovery of critical business functions across a business unit. It is the closest exercise to an actual disaster. Although a full business test requires weeks of planning and considerable coordination of personnel and resources, the exercise provides a business unit with a level of confidence about their ability to recover in an actual event.

MAINTENANCE

Most BCPs that are written are not maintained. Within a year or less the plan becomes useless because staff has changed, vendors are different, and the resources required to get the product out the door have evolved. The real shame is that in three to five years, the organization will again have to go through the entire process of creating a new plan.

By maintaining the plan on a regular basis, the organization will avoid the time required to create a plan from scratch and it will be prepared whenever a disaster strikes.

The most efficient method of maintaining the plan is to present parts of the plan to those who assisted in creating the plan initially. Team members should be verified, procedures and tasks re-examined by team members, and lists (staff, vendors, customers) updated. Any appendices such as communications schematics and computer equipment lists should be updated. Even in very large organizations, the maintenance of the plan will require a week or two of effort a year.

Index